PETER MULLEN was born and bred in the West Riding, and is now vicar of a country parish not far from York. This parish is not Marton-on-t' Moor, nor do the characters in this book exist in real life — though some of them have their remarkably similar counterparts.

PETER MULLEN

RURAL RITES

Tales of a Country Parson

TRiΔNGLE

First published 1984
Triangle/SPCK
Holy Trinity Church
Marylebone Road
London NW1 4DU

British Library Cataloguing in Publication Data

Mullen, Peter
  Rural rites.
  1. Church of England—Clergy
  I. Title
  248.8'92   BX5175

  ISBN 0-281-04127-X

Typeset by Pioneer, East Sussex.
Printed in Great Britain by
the Anchor Press, Tiptree.

CONTENTS

ACKNOWLEDGEMENTS

I would like to acknowledge the help — much of it not always appreciated by me at the time — given to me in my life and ministry by the Rev. G. N. R. Sowerby, The Rev. David Sillar, The Rev. Canon Howard Garside and the Rev. Geoffrey Allen.

And a word of thanks for Jhansi Steel who typed the manuscript.

RURAL RITES

THE STROKE OF LUCK

The wet spring had left the flat land waterlogged and so the footpath across the fields to Johnson's farm could not be walked without boots until early June. At last there came a hot, still day — a day when the heat seemed to make all nature silent, and to create again that sense of peace and timelessness which defines the English countryside. The men had at last begun haymaking and the fresh grass lay cut in the fields: damp, aromatic and bright-green.

Wilf Johnson was, in every sense, the biggest farmer for miles. His family had lived in the area since the time of the Civil War and his name was to be found all over local maps and signposts: Johnson Fold, Johnson's Cutting and, lately dilapidated and unused, Johnson's Cottage. Wilf Johnson was of the old school — that is to say he raised to the level of an unalterable principle obstinacy in work and sticking to the daily routine. Even on the day of his daughter's wedding he was supervising the early morning milking and, by evening, he was lumbering through the large barn to turn off the deafening machine that dried the corn. 'There's nowt else for it but do t'job thisel. Stuff dun't stop growin' for folks' weddins — nor milkin' neither.'

Wilf had a wooden leg. He took a grim delight in telling me how he came by it. He had been out shooting hares and, carelessly leaving his gun cocked as he crossed the stepping-stones at Bennett's brook, he had contrived to shoot himself. ''A lay theer on t'side a' t' beck for nearly an hour. Shouted but nobody din't 'ear 'owt. At finish it were Bennett 'imself wot turned up and saved mi neck. "Wilf!" 'e said, "Wilf

Johnson, by damn! Tha's covered in blood!" Well, 'a knowed
as 'a was. Warm it felt. Right warm. An' 'a was all cosy an'
sleepy — like they sez y'are when y'dyin' in t' snow on t'
mountains. "Stay where y'are", sez Stan Bennett, " 'an 'a'll
be back wi some 'elp." Well, 'a couldn't do 'owt no diff'rent
could 'a? Any road, 'a don't remember nowt else while 'a
was wakin' up in t'ospital i' York.'

His wife, the wiry Ellen with the white hair and will of
steel, nursed him in the back bedroom until he was strong
enough to grumble about not being able to get out working
in the fields. She would run up and down the stairs endlessly
with hot soup and meat and potato pie but, more often than
not, he would turn up his nose at the food and pronounce
that ''E as can't work shouldn't eat.' Whereupon Ellen
would act offended until he eventually took the tray and
began to pick at the edges of the dish.

Once harvesting began it was surprising how quickly he
recovered his appetite. But there was worse to follow: the
leg took an infection and Wilf had to return to hospital for
two more operations, partial amputations which added to
the sufferings of the household all the accumulating horror
of progressive disease. 'Gangrene. But then they reckoned
they'd stopped it. An' one mornin' t'doctor asked 'ow 'a'd
feel wi' a wooden leg. "Like yon' table", 'a said an' 'e laughed.
Any road, they fixed one up an' 'ere 'a am.'

The wooden leg worked miraculously. In six months Wilf
was out on the farm once more, a quarter of an hour at a
time to begin with, and Ellen watching him from the window
calling out for him to 'keep away from that tractor'. Two
years after that and he was running the farm as before, and
riding the tractor. He even resumed his job as sidesman at
the Sunday morning service when his regular stoop and
hobble at the end of each row made it seem as if he was
bowing to the worshippers in gratitude for their offerings.

All smart-suited and shiny shoes, he would lurch reverently towards the altar rail bearing the collecting plate.

On that June day I arrived at the Johnson farm in answer to a summons from Ellen — Wilf had suffered a stroke and was laid up again in the back bedroom. He was asleep, she said, so we might as well go through into the front room and have a cup of tea. I sat on the old sofa while Ellen, out of sight but not out of earshot, poured the kettle in the farmhouse kitchen. 'Put that cat out the front door if he's annoying you, Vicar.' Her voice sounded shrill above the rattle of the teacups. The sun dazzled through the tall window panes, lighting the old-fashioned front room with dusty beams. The dark walls held huge photographs of the Johnsons' parents and grandparents which looked down on the ornate piano with its yellowing keys. The whole room seemed unnaturally still and silent; it resembled what in fact it was — a generally unused Victorian parlour.

Ellen came in with the tray, scowling at the immaculate white cloth as if she dared it to reveal a crumb. She looked determined as ever, but there were black rings around her eyes and the startling white hair was slightly, only slightly, unkempt. ''E's a devil you know.' She talked on without a pause as she settled the tray on the polished table under the window. ''E won't pace 'imself, you see. Doesn't know when t'stop. I can't do anything with 'im. I said to 'im only last week, I said, "It's time you slowed down a bit, Wilfred Johnson; you're not as young as y'used to be." But 'e takes no notice. I told 'im 'e looked washed out. Why didn't we 'ave an 'oliday? But no. Everything was behind because of the dreadful spring an' we couldn't leave the farm. 'E stood there by that sideboard. "Nay lass", 'e said, "we've only just gotten potatoes in." I told him, "Never mind taties; when they're in they're in; there's nowt more y' can do to 'em." But 'e got on about 'aymakin' an' two of the men bein' off sick. Anyhow, the other night 'e's 'avin' a shave in t' bathroom an' a' 'ears this racket as if e'd tum'led over, like. An' when a' went in, 'e's lyin' there on t'bathroom floor all red an' 'is eyes glazed. 'E nivver moved. I thought 'e must 'ave 'ad 'eart attack or summat. Well, 'a couldn't move 'im, so I telled 'im to stay where 'e were — 'e didn't seem t'ear me — an' I'd fetch Dr Hartley. 'E was 'ere in a jiff. 'E give 'im summat an' we got 'im into bed. Doctor said it was a stroke. I didn't know what'd 'appen next. Any road, 'e's all paralysed down 'is right side. Doctor says it could be a long job.'

The delicate china cups seemed out of place in that room where everything else was so large and solid. Ellen topped up my tea and offered a cake cut into slices so huge they would not have looked out of place in a giant's parlour. She herself ate nothing. Suddenly she burst into a fit of silent crying. I had never seen her so upset before — not through all the time of Wilf's amputations and convalescence, when they were out of their minds with worry in case the surgeon had not caught the gangrene in time. She dabbed her eyes and said she was sorry for being silly. She just felt at the end of her tether. She didn't know what she was going to do with him. The doctor had said he could hear what she was saying, but there was no response. Three days and nights he had been like this. And she had not dared sleep in case she awoke to find he had died. 'It's awful, Vicar. Like 'avin' a dead body in the 'ouse. Worse than when 'e was poorly afore.'

I took her hand and held it as we sat in silence for a minute or two. She stared out of the window at the farm buildings and the road beyond with the cars seen but not heard, moving slowly up the hill. Gently I suggested that we might go upstairs and see her husband.

'There's not much point. It's like looking at somebody

who doesn't want to know you.'

Wilf filled the back bedroom with the sound of his snoring. The window was open and the breeze stirred the lace curtains. For a second I imagined they were being blown by the harsh breathing that quivered Wilf's top lip. Ellen pushed me round to the far side of the bed and then stood perfectly still watching my reactions as if I were a customer who had come to buy some of her old furniture. She said, 'Doctor says we should talk to 'im as normal like. But it seems daft when y'can tell 'e dun't 'ear nothin'.'

'Wilf! Wilf! It's me. It's the vicar of Marton come to see you. Hello Wilf. It's a grand day at last.' It was like trying to train an unco-operative parrot. In fact Wilf looked well, his huge brown face and bald head framed by the white pillow, his thick fingers entwined above the counterpane. The snores continued, alternating with Ellen's sniffs. I laid my hand gently on his forehead. 'God bless you, Wilf. We'll see you again before long.' It was like a liturgy in a waxworks. In a minute we were downstairs again.

We talked for a while longer but it was difficult to sound reassuring. Ellen recovered her composure — if that usual brisk efficiency can be called composure — and walked me to the gate. 'Thanks for cumin', Vicar. I'll let you know if anything . . . happens.' With my unshakeable belief that trauma is assuaged by routine, I thanked her for the tea and said I would call back in a day or two.

The heatwave continued over the following weekend and I was thankfully removing my dog-collar after a sticky Evensong when the phone rang.

'It's Wilf — 'e's moved! 'E's talked an' all! Well, just sort of grunted like. But 'e's comin' round. E's goin' t'be all right. Doctor says it'll take time but 'e's goin' right road.' The words came as from a war correspondent in the thick of battle. I took a can of lager from the fridge and gave silent thanks for it and for Wilf's renaissance.

It was Harvest Festival by the time the big farmer was well enough to come to church again. The Bishop came to preach at Evensong and the church was full. During the last hymn Wilf Johnson shambled up the aisle with the collecting plate. The Bishop beamed at him from behind an altar rail festooned with flowers. As our custom was, we ate the Harvest Supper in the space at the back of the church — as they had done in medieval times.

I was on my second cup of tea when Wilf limped across to where I was standing by the font. He seized my hand in his huge grip. 'Now then, Vicar. 'A was 'avin' a shave this mornin' when a right funny thought struck me. Y'know, God moves in a mysterious way . . .' I began to think it was rather late in the day for Wilf Johnson to turn pious. He continued, '. . . but y'know as 'ow 'a was paralysed down one side an' that? Y'lose all natural movement. Well, it was this side.' He leaned on a pew and raised his artificial limb '. . . an' 'a got to thinkin', if 'a 'adn't 'ad me leg off, 'a wun't a' been able t'walk!'

When he saw that I laughed, he went and told his story to the Bishop who also laughed. The rest of the evening was punctuated by the sight of Wilf Johnson approaching small groups as they nibbled the Harvest fare. The sequence was always the same: he would inveigle himself into the company, raise his wooden leg a little way as if he were a member of a decrepit chorus-line, then wait with a big rosy smile until he received the response he always knew he deserved.

2

BROADLY SPEAKING

The small rituals which surround a village funeral are evidence of a form of religion which almost goes deeper than Christianity itself. Paradoxically, they can also be occasions of irresistible comedy. In fact sometimes the ritual and the comedy are impossible to separate.

Amelia Lacey, spinster of this parish, died last autumn on a November day when the few leaves that remained on the trees in the churchyard shone like fire. There had been a frost and the path was white over as I walked among the graves to where Jack Martin was preparing Amelia's last resting place. Village grave-diggers share the inevitability of their trade. Son follows father down the years in a kind of dynastic nemesis which everyone respects because none can escape its ministrations. Perhaps that is what lent big Jack Martin's eye the cocky look as he sat on the steps by the south door and slurped tea from a pint pot.

'Mornin', Vicar. What can I do for you?' He stared at the half-dug hole in the ground, as if he were saying, 'I'll do for you one day as well.'

I said, 'I just came to make sure you knew it was a double.'

A double grave is one dug extra deep in order to accommodate more than one corpse: husband and wife, brothers, etc.

'O aye,' said Jack, 'Pilin' 'em up like dominoes again, are you?' A huge crow let out a guffaw as if in appreciation of his rustic wit. Jack finished his tea and turned reluctantly again to his shovel, smoothing the blade of it with his thick fingers, letting the wet crumbs of earth fall on to the path.

'I suppose you'd be visiting old Amelia many a time, eh Vicar?'

'Every other Thursday. She used to give me tea and tell me how much better the parish was run before the war.'

'Aye, she were a character an' all.'

She was indeed. Thin, almost frail, she was a powerhouse of energy, always on the move, houseproud, green fingers and a consummate country cook. She eyed you across her crochet as if she thought you might be about to pilfer one of her china ornaments — her 'perfect guests' as she called them. She knew everything there was to know about the history of Marton and she would recite — it was as if she had memorized a script now lost — huge chunks of it as we drank tea and consumed her cheese scones. Occasionally she would frown at her needlework and bite her lip. There would be a short silence; then the fingers would begin again as if the crochet were a commentary on her conversation. She had departed this life after a brief bout of pneumonia, aged eighty-one. The funeral arrangements were in the hands of her sister Elsie.

The church is always full for funerals but the congregation, many of whom come only on these occasions, do not bear themselves like strangers, embarrassed sheep returning briefly to the fold. On the contrary, they look entirely at home in the place, as if it had only been on loan to the Christian religion and was now being reclaimed for more significant rites. At one forty-five, the organist was quietly playing extracts from Edwardian oratorios of outstanding schmaltziness and the sidesman had lit the altar candles but had not switched on the lights; so the church looked even more eerily gothic than usual, almost you might say like a funeral parlour. I flicked every switch on the switchboard. As the lights came on, the congregation began to cough and to mutter among themselves like an audience just before curtain-up. The sidesman gave me an assured look.

'Is it wheels or bearers, Vicar?'

'Wheels, David.'

I pulled on my surplice and stepped off towards the lychgate. The cortège arrived exactly on time and the old-timers, who stood by the gate also wondering whether they would be required as bearers, stubbed out their cigarettes and stuffed their hands into overcoat pockets. Michael Derrington, the undertaker, latest in the line of disposers supreme stretching back to the time when his grandfather founded the business in the last century, stepped out on to the pavement like an impresario.

'We can't grumble for November.' As he spoke the sun came out. He caught sight of the would-be bearers. 'It's all right, lads', he said, 'I've got the wheels'. Whereupon three of the old men started up the path and the fourth shuffled off towards 'The Acorn'.

Derrington let the chief mourners out of the first car while his assistants manhandled the coffin from the hearse. Elsie Lacey, in a great black hat which reminded me of a pulpit canopy I had seen once in Leicester, stepped out on to the path. What had been lacking in the flesh of her sister she more than made up for. Her avoirdupois was legendary. She was the village metaphor for all things sizeable. But she shared her sister's liveliness — possessed it, you might say, more abundantly. There was a huge hatpin in the huge hat so that she looked as if she had been arrowed in the head. Her face was red, but it betrayed no obvious signs of grief; rather it bore an expression of critical curiosity as if suspecting trickery or foul play. Behind her were distant cousins from the East Coast.

I nodded gently and whispered, 'Good afternoon'. Elsie's critical expression never wavered. When she saw the coffin she applied a small white handkerchief swiftly to her face, then replaced it in the black and gold handbag. It was as if the movement had been a signal for the ceremonies to begin.

I led off up the path and I could hear the wheels crunching over the gravel behind and the low muttering of Derrington's men. Derrington himself made a further remark about the weather to the deceased's sister who made no reply. As we entered the porch I could hear more of the *fin de siècle* funeral music. The coffin on its aluminium trolley made me think of shopping in the Harrogate supermarket.

'I am the resurrection and the life . . .' My voice echoed through the interior and there was a clatter as the congregation rose to their feet. The service was quite straightforward. I told one or two anecdotes from my frequent visits to Amelia's cottage. I said that everyone in the village would have treasured memories of her. I said she had been a good woman and now she was at rest. We sang 'Rock of Ages' and, with Cup-Final gusto, 'Abide With Me'. During the singing it had become darker outside so that now, within, the dim lights of the nave glowed almost brightly. I stood for a minute by the chancel step and stared at the reflected light on the coffin lid, at the small cross of red flowers and at the shining brass inscription: 'Amelia Lacey RIP.' At such moments one tends to notice things very efficiently. I saw that the candles were well burned down and I made a mental note to replace them before Sunday. The organ struck up refreshingly with a march by Handel, and I led the trolley back over the soft carpet to the west door.

Outside it was dull but it still seemed brighter than the inside of the church. The sunshine had been replaced by a thin drizzle. As I rounded the Buttresses towards the south side, a crackle of plastic mackintoshes assured me that the congregation followed. Derrington held an umbrella over Elsie as the men made ready with the canvas ropes. There was a dull, solid sound of the coffin being lowered — exactly what is conveyed by the words 'earth to earth'.

Derrington ushered the mourners closer. The whole crowd of villagers stood still in the rain as if posing for a photograph. Elsie needed no encouragement to come nearer to the grave. She was at my elbow and leaning forward, her face redder than usual and having lost its habitual critical look. She seemed very distressed — and who, after all, could blame her for that, since she had lost her only near relative and she herself was approaching her departed sister's great age. Suddenly the warning words of my first vicar came rushing back. 'Always keep an eye on folks near the graveside — in case they do anything silly.' That was his euphemism for 'throwing themselves on top of the coffin.' I looked down at the brass nameplate and the handful of earth which Derrington had solemnly cast upon it. I looked back up at Elsie whose face had turned even more anxious, and who was leaning yet further over the edge. I stretched out my arm in what in the nature of the case would have been only token restraint. 'There, Elsie, she's at peace now.' It was hard to be reassuring.

The big sister stared fiercely into the grave, then drew back and faced me. The critical look had returned, intensified. The black hat had dislodged its pin and sat at a precarious angle on the side of her head. Elsie inhaled deeply and folded her arms across her chest. 'I would just like to say one thing.' She paused. Seventy mourners stood silently by, waiting upon her next words. 'She never ate a good dinner, our Amelia. I was thinking — that double grave's after being a tight fit for when it's my turn to join her.' I stuck my tongue in my cheek and pretended to stare at the tall and leafless willow tree. I could feel the force of Elsie's stare like heat on my face. At last I recovered the presence to say '. . . for they rest from their labours.' And we all went home.

3

WHO IS MY NEIGHBOUR?

Sam Bolton, who had been the keeper of the Lodge at Marton Hall, retired to a cottage on the edge of Colonel Sutter's land. It was an uneasy relationship between the Colonel and Sam. As the landed gentleman, Colonel Sutter was obviously Sam's social superior, but English rural society has ways and means of declaring a servant greater than his master. The chief consideration is historical continuity of occupations. You see, Sam's father had been lodge-keeper at Marton Hall and so Sam had grown up on the estate. Since he was a quarter of a century older than his present landlord, Sam often found himself in the advantageous position of being able to reminisce in public about the master's childhood. There was nothing so demeaning for the Colonel as to find himself, towards the sleepy end of a parish get-together, regaled by the well-drunk Sam's half remembrances of things past. 'I recollect when the Colonel fell in the lake and came out without his short pants . . .'

Sam would sit in the corner, screwing up his eyes against his pipe smoke, resting his foot on his old dog. Striped-trousered Colonel Sutter would draw heavily on all the powers of self-abnegation bred into the race of English gentlemen and smile a plastic smile in the direction of Sam's joke. With studied ambiguity he would reply, 'Where would Marton be without Old Sam?' Then he would down his brandy and bid everyone good-night. I never thought there was actual ill will in these exchanges, but there was always a certain edge to Sam's remarks and to the tone of Roger Sutter's responses, which betrayed something of the acrimony of the old master-servant relationship. The trouble was that Sam — and more importantly, Sam's father — had worshipped Roger's father. The father was a genial country-man who had spent hours walking his estate and had the leisure and perspicacity to take his staff into his confidence, ask their advice and so on. Unlike him, Roger had spent all his time away from home in the army, so that to the locals he appeared as a fêted visitor, an aloof outsider who now and then deigned to honour Marton Hall with his presence. Moreover, he was unmarried.

The 'Old Squire' died and his son retired from the army in order to look after the estate. He was an honest, fair-minded man but one who, doubtless because of his army training, had a brusqueness of manner which the estate staff, and Sam in particular, divined as arrogance. Retired army officers are posted all over the English countryside and usually in the finest houses, but their relationship with the locals is nearly always uneasy. Somehow the farmers and the labourers have discerned that the military men owe allegiance, not to what is local and therefore 'real', but to some other distant hierarchy which knows nothing of the land and so cannot have the interests of countrymen at heart. All those retired majors, colonels and brigadiers are tolerated by the locals, respected, even, in a cool and dutiful fashion. But duty is a poor substitute for affection, and the military men inhabit the countryside like sentries outside the gates.

I called to see Colonel Sutter one day in the middle of July. The long curving drive was being resurfaced and I was held up by the big yellow machine which poured forth the pungent sticky tar. The grounds were at their best: a hundred and eighty acres of meadow and woodland around the ornamental lake. Marton Hall itself, a twenty-six room eighteenth-century mansion, stood foursquare on the hill,

surrounded with poplars. It made you think of wigs, Mr.
D'Arcy and the *Eine Kleine Nachtmusik* — but not while
the resurfacing machine exuded its throaty din, and jet
trainers from the local RAF Station thundered below the
clouds.

'Peter! Do come in. I'm so glad you could come. I don't
know when they'll finish. Were you held up long?' He
scowled at the bright yellow machine now silent as the
workmen stretched out on the grass over mugs of tea. We
went into the music room. It seemed to be full of — actually
there were only two — harpsichords and ancestral portraits.
Roger's grandparents stared down piercingly from the east
wall. They looked severe, preoccupied — the sort of faces
you could imagine on playing card royals. High-ranking
officers glared back at them from a couple of military
magazines on the low oak table. Quality begets quietness.
The only sound in that bright room was of Roger pouring
whisky. Quality is heavy cut glass. I sat in the broad wicker
chair and he stood by the grandfather clock as if he had just
sprung out of it.

'Briefly' he said, 'I wanted to have a word with you about
Old Sam.' He winced and took a sip of his whisky. 'It's all
very embarrassing. You'll have noticed I've been thinning
the trees on the estate. Well, I had those two elms by
Bolton's fence removed and now he's threatening to sue
me.' The clock struck three and the Colonel sat down.

'I suppose you mentioned to Sam what you planned?'

'That's just it. He was in hospital at the time — that
operation on his waterworks. I was in a hurry. The contractor
offered me a deal on all the work that needed doing, so I
told him to go ahead. Then I received a visit from Sam
Bolton, followed by his solicitor's letter threatening legal
action.' He went to refill the glasses. I gazed out over the
lawn at a large Persian cat squeezing itself through a croquet

hoop. I said, 'As far as the legal aspect goes, there's nothing in it, is there? There can't be, really, since it's your land.' 'Unfortunately, there's some doubt even about that. My father made some sort of deal with old Mr Bolton — Jim, Sam's father — about his retirement and that cottage. No one's quite sure how much land was attached to it at the time of transfer. The original deeds were destroyed in an air raid.'

'There must be some way you could make it up to Sam. I mean, the damage is done but perhaps . . .'

'I've thought of that. I've tried. It was so embarrassing. Humiliating. I thought "Now, what would father have done?" So I went down to see Sam — a social call if you like. He was leaning over the gate with a belligerent expression on his face. Well, he invited me in at last but with such suspicion. I might have been the Trojan horse. We sat by the fire and he kept half-shutting his eyes and blowing that foul pipe smoke until the room was misty. I tell you, I was so embarrassed I didn't know what to say. In the end I said quite the wrong thing. I offered to do the cottage up for him. I might have been threatening him with murder. He hammered his pipe against the chimney breast; then he stood up and said that if there were anything needed doing with his own cottage he would do it himself, and he hadn't invited me in so that I could insult him and so on. I retreated, apologizing profusely.'

He stood silently by the window. I said, 'I could have a word with Sam — if you think it will do any good. Not that I have any special influence there, but he used to sing in the choir, did Sam, when he was younger. And his father was a sidesman for thirty years.'

Roger sat down again. He looked relieved. I told him I could not promise spectacular results but he still looked unburdened like an earnest penitent at absolution. We walked slowly towards the door, our voices echoing in the hall loudly enough to disturb the dogs. As we passed the passage that leads to the kitchen there came the sound of shattering crockery followed by a throaty expletive. Roger raised his eyebrows and smiled, 'You see', he said 'there's a jinx on the place!' We shook hands at the door and he thanked me again in advance for my offer to intercede with Sam.

The workmen had finished for the day and their machines lay like huge extinct reptiles on either side of the drive. There was a strong smell of tar and the path sparkled in the sunlight. I thought I saw someone moving by the Lodge gate. As I drew closer I recognized the bulky figure of Sam Bolton staggering all over the drive. He looked ill. I stopped the car and ran after him. If the scent of his breath did not tell the whole story, certainly the style of his speech did. 'Ah, Vicar! It's my old friend the Vicar! Sorry I can't offer you a drink, Vicar, but I've drunk it all.'

He began to sing 'I've drunk it all' over and over again in parody of the hymnal. His dog offered an apologetic look. 'Come on Sam, you'll get yourself knocked down. Let me give you a lift home.'

He stood with his feet still, his knees swaying, and fixed me with a stare reminiscent of the Ancient Mariner. 'Knock down? Knock down?' he repeated as if it were the second verse of his sacrilegious hymn. 'I'll knock him down. Too right I'll knock him down!' Nonetheless he fell into the car. As soon as his head hit the back of the passenger seat he became calmer. His face took on an amiable, dazed expression. 'This is a nice car, Vicar. It's nice and warm in here.' The dog settled in the back. I leaned across him and pulled the door shut. 'That's right, Sam, you settle down and I'll drive you home.'

'Sorry I can't offer you a drink, Vicar. I've drunk it all.' He gave the words tragic import, then lapsed into silence. Five minutes later I pulled up outside his cottage. The journey seemed to have refreshed him, and, as soon as he realized he was back on his own territory, he began again his flurry of gesticulation. 'See there! See — them stumps is where my elms was — that's what! My trees, my own trees!' It would have made fine melodrama.

After considerable persuasion he consented to get out of the car and with more cajoling he eventually — after a minor crisis concerning the whereabouts of his door key — entered the cottage. I sat him in his armchair and made some strong coffee. He gazed at the blue and white mug for a long time as if he suspected poison, then his head fell forward and he was asleep. I fetched the stool for his feet and the melancholy dog lay down by the side of his chair. I found a scrap of paper and a pencil.

'Sam, your coffee has gone cold! — Peter Mullen, vicar of Marton'.

Two days later there was a phone call from Roger Sutter. 'I just want to thank you for everything.'

After a bit of fairly tactful probing, it turned out that Sam and the Colonel had got together and, as it were, signed the truce. And when the garden party was held at Marton Hall, Sam Bolton was supervising the beer tent as usual — with, if it were possible, even more enthusiasm than ever. Colonel Sutter never mentioned the issue of the trees again but the following spring I noticed three new saplings bending before the north wind on the edge of the circular path that divides Sam Bolton's back lawn from the estate proper. Nearby there was a small plaque: 'Planted in affectionate memory of James Bolton (1894-1976) a loyal friend of Marton Hall.'

4

THE VISIT

One year we enjoyed — I'm sure that is the right word — a visit from students with their Vice-Principal from the theological college. It was an education for the parishioners of St Luke's since, like everyone else, they had never bothered to wonder where parsons actually came from. And so I was obliged to take them on one side and, as it were, relieve them of the vaguely superstitious idea that the clergy are born into the cloth, or else that they are visited upon the people as a shocking punishment for various naughtinesses. 'You see, they are taught the Bible and doctrine and history in the college, but they have to be allowed to come out and practise for a bit before the Bishop lays hands on them.' I felt like a father explaining the birds and the bees.

The college might have been Castle Dracula for all the contact locals had had with it in the past. It looked a weird place, set apart in its own grounds between the edge of the farmland and the coast. And when the lights appeared in upstairs windows on winter nights, you would have imagined religion as the last explanation for what was taking place inside. But now there was a new regime: old Canon Beresford-Walker, who had ruled the place like one of the Egyptian taskmasters, retired, and one of the church's new breed of relevant communicators was put in. This was the Rev. Stuart Holmes, a dapper cleric who nipped about the place in a little sports car and — to the enormous delight of the locals — bowled demon leg-breaks for the village cricket team. Whereas the old Canon had visited the local church only rarely, perhaps to conduct an early morning Communion Service during my annual holiday or to talk to Farmer Jackson about a strip of glebe land that belonged to the college, the Rev. ('Call me Stuart') Holmes was forever buzzing in and out of the local shops and even in the village pub.

'When we saw him in here supping a pint the other lunchtime, Vicar, we thought you'd been replaced', said Sam Bolton. Apparently one of the Principal's chief skills was dominoes, of the species known as 'Fives and Threes', and this occupation drew him often to the parlour at The Acorn.

Still, we knew little about the students until one evening over supper in the vicarage Stuart leaned across the table and said, 'Look, Peter, we could come and take over the parish for a few weeks if you like. Preach your sermons. Visit the sick and the old folk. What d'you say?' I didn't say anything for a while, contriving to conceal my doubts behind a lengthy chew at a gristly piece of lamb. As he waited for my response, the Principal was arranging the knives and forks, the salt and pepper assiduously, as if he were ordering the parish already.

'Well, I suppose . . .', I began.

He was very enthusiastic. 'It would give the students a taste of the real thing. They're all theory you know. Theology in a vacuum. Philosophy and text books about preaching. And they all think they're going to convert the whole world once they're ordained. Now, you let them come in and see parish life in the raw and you'll be doing them a great service.'

I was rather uncertain about his reference to Marton as 'in the raw' but it seemed a good idea in theory. I looked across at my wife, Barbara, but her face gave away nothing except a faint smile as she folded her napkin and asked, 'Who's for

ice cream?' The Rev. Stuart Holmes was for ice cream. He
was also for visiting his students upon us at the earliest
opportunity. 'In the autumn. Harvest Festivals and the like.
Let them see country life as it is. Some of our lot come from
so deep in the towns their natural element is carbon
monoxide.' Without a pause he called out to Barbara '. . .
strawberry *and* chocolate — if I may have just a teeny-
weeny bit of both.'

Shortly before the visit was due to take place, I received a
letter — on the swish new college-printed notepaper —
informing me that the Rev. Stuart Holmes very much
regretted he would not himself be able to accompany the
students on the visitation. His presence was commanded at
some international conference of principals in New York.
Of course, if the choice were his — but, unfortunately, it
was not, etc. We would, he was sure, give an equally warm
welcome to the Vice-Principal, the Rev. Dominic O'Grady.

They all arrived — twenty students and the chain-smoking
O'Grady — one Wednesday morning towards the end of
September. I will not say that the next few weeks were like
the days of tribulation prophesied for the end of time, those
days which, unless the Lord shorten them, no one will be
able to bear; but the experience was, as the Chinese say,
'interesting'. Rural England is extreme in its dislike of
extremes and, as might have been expected, the Rev.
Dominic O'Grady struck them as being very extreme indeed.
He was a small man, thin, with a pale face and a high-
pitched voice, not born in Ireland, but in Rochdale,
Lancashire. The students had been known to refer to him as
'Matchstick Man'. He always wore his cassock, which was in
the Roman style and known in the trade as a 'thirty-niner',
buttoned from neck to ankle. The moderate lapsed Protes-
tants of Marton saw him instantly as a papal fifth columnist
in their midst. The everlasting cigarette in his mouth and

the ash down his black frontage were his trademarks. Duffield the organist called him 'Holy Smoke'.

We held a briefing in the study. The students were given names and addresses of parishioners whom they would visit, a dozen apiece, all sorts and conditions from the devout to the spiritually deaf. One of our students was missing and he phoned up during the meeting to say he had caught chicken pox. He also had no change for the pay phone in the college, so he reversed the charges. Half an hour later there was another phone call – good wishes for the visitation from Stuart Holmes in America. I was thankful *he* had not reversed charges.

The students were nervous and excitable, covering their apprehensiveness with noisy clatter and gratuitous giggles every time the Vice-Principal made a half-joke. Of sixteen men and four girls, the youngest was about twenty, the oldest, a former salesman with a shiny head, in his fifties. A young man and a girl – they obviously shared more than merely collegiate affection – stayed behind to wash the coffee cups. Barbara came in and they asked her what it was like being a vicar's wife. She said that in Marton it was much like being a vicar. 'They put great importance on women having their own career in college nowadays', said the girl whose own career ambitions were vicar-shaped, if ever the good old C. of E. gets round to ordaining women. 'Women aren't just expected to do the flowers and run the Mothers' Union and that. Not nowadays.' Barbara said we didn't have a Mothers' Union in Marton, 'And you're only allowed to do the flowers in these parts if you're an expert – which I'm not.' With that she went off to get ready for her afternoon's teaching in St Luke's (Junior Mixed and Infants) C. of E. (Controlled).

Three weeks later we all met again in the study to say our farewells. They looked like soldiers having returned to the comparative safety of the trenches after the heat of battle. Illusions, if not entirely shattered by the visitation, had at least received a few civilizing indentations. Most of them were going out with more than they came in with — bodily as well as spiritually. Parishioners, proud of their country cuisine, had vied with one another to provide for their guests. The services had been well-attended and the presence of so many eligible young men at the Harvest Dance had brought a frisson of romance such as the village hall had not felt since the war when the Yanks were stationed just outside Marton.

But there were those among the visitors who looked disapprovingly upon such fleshpots. These were the evangelical revivalist phalanx, three men and a girl of the most serious-minded religious commitment, who had decided that their stay in Marton should, under the Lord, achieve nothing less than the conversion of the whole village from its naughty ways to the clear light of the Kingdom. All the students lodged with members of the congregation and, as it happened, Elspeth the enormous evangelical was staying at the vicarage. The second morning I stepped, all unknowing, into the bathroom only to encounter her looming naked out of the steaming mist like one of the demons her preaching was meant to warn against. She was not at all discomfited by my intrusion but flashed me a smile across the toothpaste and called out 'Morning, brother! Isn't it glorious? Praise the Lord!' While I was still trying to loosen my tongue, the glory clutching a green towel slithered past me and off down the corridor singing 'Bind us together in love'. I was surprised that one so obviously healthy as Elspeth never ate breakfast. She was always out of the house by a quarter to nine in search of her three zealous companions who were all staying at the Duffields' old house opposite the pub.

Michael Duffield is the church organist. Like most of his

kind he rates his own contribution to the act of corporate worship rather higher than the vicar's. In fact he considers it a wonderful act of magnanimity on his part to allow the vicar to conduct the service at all — that is, to interrupt the natural flow of music with all those tedious words of banns, notices and sermonizing. But if, on a cool evening, he begins to blow on his fingers and stumble about on his pedals when the vicar's sermon exceeds the ten and a half minutes allowed by the Organists' Union, imagine his reaction when the sermon lasts a full half hour; moreover when it is preached not by the vicar, nor even by a member of the much reviled species of curates, but by a mere — though 'mere' has only a figurative meaning in this case — woman such as Elspeth Reynolds.

The whole service on the last evening was to be conducted by the students. Michael hurtled into my vestry five minutes before it was due to start. Seeing the ensurpliced Elspeth by my side, he glared so fiercely I thought he would crack his bifocals. 'Who's responsible for this order of service? I might as well not be here. Five hymns you've got, and four of them to *guitar* — he spoke the word as if it were a foul taste on the tongue — accompaniment.' Elspeth gave him a born-again smile. 'For the young people's sake Mr. Duffield. The Lord brings forth from his treasures both old and new, you know.'

Duffield's eyes darted about the vestry as if in search of some neutral object upon which they could settle unoffended. 'Oh aye? Well, the Lord has always managed without guitars before. And what's this?' — he smacked the Order of Service with the back of his hand — ' "there will follow an interlude during which members of the college will dance the Gospel." I've heard of dancing at wakes in Ireland. But this is England, Miss — the Church of England, not the London Palladium!'

Her smile broadened. 'Wakes, Mr Duffield? Yes, that's what we hope to do. Wake up the congregation to the Good News . . .'

'Good news? I haven't heard any good news!'

'Gospel, Mr Duffield. "Gospel" means good news.'

He was gesticulating like a traffic cop. 'So it's take your partners for the parable of the sower is it? Excuse me Mr Herod, could I have the pleasure of this foxtrot —'

'Something like that.'

The vestry clock, like a referee, called time. 'Come on', I said, turning off the fluorescent light strip, 'or we'll be late.' Duffield slipped through the side door to his organ seat, limping like a wounded fox. Elspeth followed him, her spruced face shining like light from the glorious Kingdom. When the choirboys saw her they chirruped and snuffled behind their hands until John Wedgard the tenor began the vestry prayer, as he generally did, in a tinny staccato voice as if he were giving information about the train now arriving on platform seven. The procession meandered into the church to the boisterous hymn, 'Trumpet of God sound high, till the hearts of the heathen shake' (*Ancient and Modern* (revised) number 270), an eccentric choice but not mine. As soon as we were in our places, Elspeth's three friends began to introduce the service. Their technique seemed to owe less to theological training and more to the art of television presentation. 'Dearly beloved brethren' became, from the mouth of the tall, pimpled student in the 'Jesus Saves' T-shirt, 'Hi there, folks!' Then began the first strains of the liturgical guitars — three boys and two girls bobbing about on the chancel step singing,

'We're gonna sing to Jesus (*clap*)
We're gonna sing to Jesus (*clap*)
We're gonna sing (*clap clap*)

We're gonna sing (*clap clap*)
We're gonna sing to Jesus (*clap clap clap clap . . .*)'

Then Duffield's nightmare started:

'We're gonna dance to Jesus (*clap*)
We're gonna etc . . .'

At once the chancel was filled with young girls who gospel-danced in a most uninhibited style. This was certainly good news for the more precocious choirboys whose only previous glimpse of the mobile female form in church had been Ethel Lister's nine-year-old daughter as Zipporah in the story of Moses. Another student in jeans with braces stood in the pulpit and cajoled the packed congregation into rhythmic clapping. After this an acted parable: the Prodigal Son. Elspeth read from a version of the Bible that sounded like a manual for hippies. Various students mimed the Prodigal's sojourn in the far country. I thought the 'riotous living' was particularly authentic, though even from where I was sitting I could feel the discomfiture of Mrs Hirst and her colleagues from the Women's Circle about five rows back. Beyond all the jigging about by the spindly young men and the nubile young women, certain phrases from that revised translation sounded oddly: 'riotous living' itself became 'a real lit-up time' and 'bring hither the fatted calf' was transmogrified into 'rustle up the biggest joint we've got in the ice-box, man.' I risked a glance at Duffield. He was leaning far back in his seat, arms folded, eyes fixed on the roof, lips curled in a silent whistle. More guitars and —

'A sinner came back, came back, came back
A sinner came back again,
A sinner returned to his father's house
A sinner no more to remain.'

At last it was time for the sermon. Elspeth hauled herself into the pulpit and began the process of convicting the easy-going burghers of Marton of their sin. We were all like that Prodigal. We had all betrayed Our Father's trust and so on. The choirmen began to doze. The boys began to fidget. The congregation coughed, jingled their collection, fumbled with their bits and pieces. Occasionally a prayer book would clatter to the floor. In short it was just like a normal sermon, but preached with a sort of ecstatic glee and littered with anecdotes — some of which even I had heard before. The Vice-Principal looked as if he had heard them too. He sat tense on the front row, fingering the front of his thirty-niner. I could tell he was dying for a smoke. As Frenchmen talk with their hands, Elspeth preached with her eyebrows. They wriggled about her forehead like caterpillars. Later, counting the collection in the vestry, old Jack Reid got a snigger out of his fellow sidesmen by saying 'I thought, ay up lad, she's mekkin eyes at yer!'

After half an hour of the good news of our damnation, the lady preacher soared to her climax — but not hers only, for every one of us was to join in a loud proclamation of 'Father, forgive me; I have sinned.' We had to repeat this, pantomime style, three times until the preacher thought we shouted loud enough to sound sincere. But if many found that sort of trained penitence faintly embarrassing, it was as nothing to the commotion about to be loosed among the congregation.

A young man rushed into the chancel noisily and threw his arms around a girl who had been specially put there for that purpose. Obviously it was more of the godly mime. Elspeth supplied the commentary. 'You see, folks, God wants us to do more than simply go down on our knees and confess to him. He wants us to say we're sorry to our neighbours as well. So I want all of you to turn to your neighbour — go ahead now, to the person next to you in the pew, put your arms around his or her neck and say, 'Brother (or sister of course as the case may be) I have sinned against you, too, and I'm sorry.'

All over the church this was done with varying degrees of commitment ranging from the half-hearted to the genuinely apathetic — except by the sidesmen in the raised seats on the back row who merely looked at each other with that hapless look that they used when someone revoked at dominoes in 'The Acorn'. Bert Harrison, the rotund bass who also kept the gardening store, put a hand on my shoulder, grinned at me and said, 'I'll get young Timothy to fetch you those seeds round in the morning, Vicar.' For small mercies I was exceedingly thankful. The next part of the action sent me stiff with terror. I though I would be turned into a pillar of salt for, as I looked back towards the pulpit, I saw Elspeth with a look of saving affection on her face lunging lustily towards the organ. Michael Duffield had decided to take no further part in hostilities and so, seizing upon the thought that the general schmaltzy confession could do with a bit of musical accompaniment, he had let his fingers wander idly over the silent keys. Suddenly, from behind, the mighty penitence of Elspeth was flung around his neck, followed by the loud utterance of 'Brother, I have sinned, etc.' Michael just carried on playing. He was like a captain clinging to his wheel while the ship sank. Elspeth hung upon him like a life jacket. I wondered whether she would keep him in the spiritual half-Nelson until he removed his fingers from the keyboard in capitulation. But he did no such thing and eventually she was forced to release him from her affection. Duffield switched off the mechanism and the organ died with a whirr and a wheeze. Then he slipped off through the side panel and a moment later I heard the vestry door slam shut. We walked out in silence and I excused myself from the 'Marton Youth for Christ' discotheque that the students had arranged in the church hall. I found Duffield in 'The Acorn' half way down his second pint. 'Have one y'self, Vicar. When are they off back, that lot — tomorrow is it?'

Tomorrow it was. Before they all left the Vice-Principal made a short speech, exuding gratitude and smoke. The senior student presented the parish with a copy of the swinging Bible they had used the night before. Then they all wandered out on to the lawn. All except Elspeth who, if rather resigned or even chastened, but calm for once, thanked Barbara and me for our hospitality. 'Don't think of my going as losing a lodger; think of it as gaining a bathroom instead.' She smiled a sweet non-religious smile, then handed me a paper bag with the trademarks of Handley's Music Shop down the side. 'Will you give this to Mr Duffield for me, please? I think he's a lovely man and I wouldn't do anything in the world to hurt him.' She blushed and then disappeared abruptly out on to the lawn. When she had gone I had a peep inside the bag. It contained a book of organ solos by Walford Davies — some of Duffield's very favourites.

I went outside and said goodbye to the students, said that perhaps we might see some of them again another year. It was a quarter past twelve. It was a warm day for early October. I knew where I would find my organist. A half pint would make a nice accompaniment to Elspeth's musical offering.

5

COMPLICATED GROUND

When we moved to this parish I was showing an old friend round the vicarage. In the chief bedroom he scowled suddenly and turned away from the window. 'Ugh! I don't know how you can bring yourself to sleep in a room overlooking a graveyard.'

'Why not?' I said. 'I think you've been watching too many horror films. This is Marton, not Transylvania you know. English graveyards are homely, not sinister.'

He stared out over the haphazard crosses in the long grass and shook his head. 'Not for me, thanks. But I must say I do like that.' He pointed to the huge statue of an angel holding a scroll. 'Now that's the sort of memorial I wouldn't mind on my own grave.'

'Yes, but at today's prices it would cost you about six thousand pounds. Anyhow the diocesan authorities wouldn't allow it.'

As we were talking I noticed a little girl in a bright-yellow dress wandering about among the gravestones. She stood for a long while by a neglected grave upon which stood a rusty, empty vase. Then she bent to pick a handful of daisies and dandelions which she arranged neatly in the vase. She stood back with her arms folded and admired her handiwork.

'What d'you mean, the diocese wouldn't allow me my angel?' We stepped out onto the landing and a salvo of aggressive pop music met us from the kitchen below.

'Turn that down, Karl, please.'

Above the pop: 'Pardon?'

I shouted back, 'I said please turn it down.' The din ceased halfway through my sentence and I was left shrieking at the silence.

'OK, there's no need to shout. I'm going out now, Dad.' The slamming of the back door was followed by cheerfully tuneless whistling from the garden.

My friend and I recommenced a familiar mutual grouse about young people not seeming to be interested in anything that did not appear in the Top Twenty. 'Weren't we all like that once, though?' he said, running the palm of his hand over the balcony as if in recollection of his own youthful adventures. 'Anyhow, you were explaining why I can't have an angel on my tombstone.'

I led him into the study and took down the diocesan handbook. Page forty-seven, Regulation 16 (Churchyards): 'Only certain specifications of memorials are permitted. No kerbs. No extravagant figures. No open books.'

'Bureaucrats! Spoilsports!'

'That's nothing. Turn over the page.'

He read: 'Crosses: these are to be discouraged as they represent undue repetition of the supreme Christian symbol.' He paused. 'No,' he said, 'You're having me on. This isn't the — what is it? — the diocesan regulations. It's a spoof, eh? One of your Karl's jokes. The Monty Python version of the C. of E.'

I assured him it was not. He laughed louder than the offending pop music. 'Undue repetition of the supreme Christian symbol! Ha! I can just see members of your diocesan committee descending in pinstripes and pique on the war cemeteries in France. "Ah, Monsieur Archdeacon, ne touchez pas le croix s'il vous plait!" "Mais je regrette, madame, la commission a dit . . ." Peter, you must cut it out and lend it to *Private Eye*. What bureaucracy! It beats the Common Market. Hey, you could start an EEC crucifix mountain with all the unwanted crosses!'

He looked at the kitchen clock and said it was time he went home. When he switched on the car ignition, sedate pop of the Swinging Sixties exuded from the cassette on the dashboard. He gave me a sheepish look and turned down the volume before driving off.

It was early June. The churchyard was all bright colours among long grass, the blazing start to the busy rural summer. The heat and the extravaganza of the grass and the wild flowers set the churchyard aside as an indolent, timeless place. The old men would sit in the sun on the south side and talk over old times until the end of August. The path from the lychgate was speckled by cherry blossom brought down in Wednesday night's storm. It looked like confetti.

I found the little girl in the yellow dress sitting silently on one of the kerbstones that were officially disapproved of. She looked thoughtful.

'Good afternoon! Have you finished collecting flowers?'

She jumped up suddenly and overturned the rusty vase. 'Oh, I was only picking the wild flowers.'

'I know you were.' I helped her replace the daisies and dandelions in the vase.

'I often come in here. I like to think. It's nice and quiet.' She was about seven. I was on the edge of repenting about my criticism of young people as having heads stuffed with nothing but pop music when she said, 'What are graves really for?'

How to explain without giving her my friend's phobia of cemeteries! 'They're for memorials. That grave you put flowers on. That's a memorial — in memory of someone who's died.'

'And are they really in them, all the people — in the graves?' The ribbons which held her plaits were shaped like the forbidden crosses. She sat down again and rubbed her fingers over the inscription on the edge of the kerb: 'Emily Hayes 1818-1893 RIP.'

'Why does it say "rip"?'

'It's not "rip" really. It's initials. Short for "rest in peace".' She asked several more questions while I was still struggling to answer her first one. I managed to explain that when people died and went to God they did not need their old bodies any more, so these were brought into church to a funeral where all the people could give thanks for the life of their friend. Afterwards — and only because the old bodies were no use any longer — the dead person was put in his grave.

'Some of the dead people get forgotten though, don't they?' She gazed at the grave she had been tending. There were bird droppings on the headstone and the marble chips — or what was left of them — were piled up unevenly between the kerbs.

'Well, even the sons and daughters of the very old people have to die some time. Look at Emily Hayes here. She died in 1893. I shouldn't think there'll be anyone alive today who remembers her.'

She did not seem at all upset, and we had a long talk after that. She told me her name was Lesley. When it was time to go, we walked across the middle of the graveyard to the little gate in the far corner near the yew tree. We passed a very superior Victorian grave with iron railings and an obelisk. Lesley wanted to know why it was bigger than all the others. I said it must mark the resting place of someone who was reckoned to have been very important. She said, 'God is very important isn't he?'

Naturally the Vicar agreed.

Suddenly she looked up, shielding her eyes against the sun, and pointed towards the church. She spoke very confidently: 'I know that's God's grave. But it doesn't say his name on it. Is that because no one remembers him?'

Out of the mouths of babes and sucklings. . . .

6

SWEET SUNDAY

It was so hot that the cows simply stood still in the fields,
with scarcely the energy to flick the flies away. The old folk
leaned against doorposts, almost ready to concede that the
weather was as good as it had always been in the good old
days when, as Mrs Moreton, frail, freckled and white-haired,
used to say, 'You could fry an egg on the pavement and read
a newspaper on the doorstep at eleven o'clock at night.' A
hot Sunday in the English countryside is, with the single
exception of snow, the only natural phenomenon to make
villagers change their routine. It is a psychological as well as
a physical change. People bring chairs into the garden and
sit dazzled over the newspapers while the socially avant-
garde even take their meals outside. The village pub entirely
changes its character as tin seats and striped umbrellas are
dragged on to the car park so that tourists from the towns
can enjoy the fresh air and the rural scenery while they
shout at their children. But anyone tempted to conclude
from all this that the stiff English have finally accepted the
style of the Continental Sunday had better think again; for
while Europeans and other foreigners merely enjoy themselves when the weather is fair, the English cling fast to their
puritanism and their guilt. So when folks bring out their
chairs and their cold drinks they do so uneasily, with
embarrassment. And if you happen to pass by one of the
gardens and call out a greeting, the shamefaced occupants
will always reply with some mark of their distaste for
enjoyment, like, 'It's too hot,' or 'We've only just come out.'
It is not, after all, a holiday; it is only Sunday. Those who

attend church in such weather do so with an especial sense of abstinence and their smiles as you meet them at the church door seem to say, 'There. You didn't think I'd be put off by a little sunshine — like some I could mention!'

At exactly twelve o'clock church is over and the rites of atonement begin. These feature all kinds of gardening tools and the sight of people of all ages suffering joyfully as they bend over weeds and the cabbage patch. But the favourite device for proclaiming one's industriousness is the lawn-mower. These are the outward and visible signs of the Calvinist conscience. To be seen pushing a lawnmower on a hot Sunday afternoon is to belong to the company of the saved; and a non-electrified, non-oil machine is the very mark of sanctity. The sound of the mowers acts like a call to prayer, and the resistance of even the most persistent unbeliever is eventually broken down. So by mid-afternoon the workaday peace and quiet of the village is replaced by a loud discordant drone from which there is no escape except by going back into the house and closing all the windows. The din persists until Evensong. I had not thought there was so much grass. How peaceful, by comparison, must be the dark satanic mills of the town on the idle sabbath.

It is a relief to go to Evensong for a spell of quiet timelessness, with the sun streaming through the coloured lights of the high west window, the organ accompaniment to a form of religion which is sempiternally English, the final hymn, 'The Day Thou Gavest, Lord, is Ended'. Except it is not ended: when you come out you are met by the snap-jaw sound of hedge-clippers or the last fading drone of the recalcitrant mower, the man-a-mow, goaded by the noise of industry until he could stand it no longer, striding ill-tempered over the grass, his back flayed red by the sun — just recompense for his indolent afternoon.

After Evensong we set out on our usual walk past the end

of the village and into the quiet fields and cool woodland.
The summer evening light in these parts is often hazy, and
as the sun descends over the yellowing fields the whole
county looks like an impressionist painting. Except that, on
that particular evening, we did not get as far as the fields. As
we passed the Mickleovers', a bee flew in under the lens of
my glasses. Startled, I brushed it away only to feel the
buzzing of several more around my head. I glanced at
Barbara and saw that she too was flailing about, trying to
beat off the noisy insects. Soon there were too many to beat
off and we realized we were being attacked by at least part
of the swarm. Instinctively we ran and, as we turned the
corner near the Jarretts' greenhouse, a company of people
taking drinks on the lawn stared at us as if we were some
sort of bizarre entertainment. Oddly, I seemed to notice
their every unconcerned move: the way a young lad in jeans
and T-shirt popped peanuts in his mouth, Michael Jarrett
lighting a cigarette, Aunt Bess from next door sipping from
a glass of lemonade. Then I felt the bees stinging under my
shirt. My hair was alive with them in a loud and continuous
buzzing like one of the accursed lawnmowers. My face felt
uncomfortably hot as if I had sat too close to the fire. We ran
as victims in a nightmare, breathless and with heavy limbs,
unable to put distance between ourselves and our tormen-
ters. Barbara accidentally stepped into the road and was
almost knocked down by a shiny black vintage car, the
driver staring nonplussed out of the open top. Suddenly an
astronaut stood gesticulating in our path. It was Keith
Mickleover in his bee-keeper's outfit and waving a spray
gun. I thought we were saved at last, but he only mouthed
panic under his visor as we ran past. 'What shall we do?' I
called out, the demons still jabbing at my flesh. 'Run like
hell!' was Mickleover's muted advice from behind the
perspex. I grabbed Barbara's hand at the third attempt. We

fled like damned spirits but, as with them, so with us; there was no escape.

The last house in the village lay about a hundred yards ahead. I saw it as our only hope but all our running seemed to bring it no nearer. Gradually I began to make out a figure standing at the gate. It was old Mrs Kenyon. We had buried her husband last March. Obscurely I remembered we sang 'Abide With Me' at his funeral. Mrs Kenyon was smiling at us as if charging through the village — though generally it would be thought undignified in a man of the cloth — might be excused at the end of a hot day. Her face changed as she realised our terror was not feigned. Seconds later we were safely seated in her darkened parlour, the buzz of the bees abated, the only sound over our breathlessness the sporadic twittering of the old lady's budgerigar. Mrs Kenyon, calm in a crisis, emerged from the kitchen with tea and advice that the best thing for bee stings is bicarbonate of soda and honey. She said nothing for a long time, then all at once asked, 'Are you all right?' The television set had been left on with the sound turned down. The smiling newsreader introduced scenes of summer sports and the crowded seaside.

Soon we felt fit enough to make our way home and we escaped from Mrs Kenyon's hospitable recommendation of sodium bicarbonate and ammonia. 'And don't forget to take some honey.' Villagers stood at their doors in the warm evening as if the whole street were lined with folk to welcome heroes back from the wars. There were more words of advice. Once back at the vicarage I telephoned Dr Stead immediately. His wife said he had called into 'The Acorn' for a glass of lager. She would get him to pop in on the way home. Half an hour later he sat sipping scotch with us, having brought forth antihistamine tablets which 'you were lucky I had in the car'.

We were sore for days but we were assured by all and sundry that as a result of our experience we would never suffer from rheumatism, that it was a sign of blessing to be stung by bees and that if we made sure to get all the stings out the red blotchiness would soon subside. More shocked by the event than ourselves were the Mickleovers who rang while Dr Stead was still with us to offer their own anti-histamine 'which we always keep by us being as we're in the business' and to explain that Keith had just happened to remove the covers from a hive as we were passing. Apparently bees are affected by hot weather.

As we sat out on the unmown lawn on Tuesday afternoon, the sabbath heat persisting through the octave, Sally Mickleover appeared at the gate. She had brought us six jars of honey as compensation for the thousand natural shocks. As we spread it thickly on the toast at teatime it seemed like sweet revenge.

7

THE ORDINAND

Marton has not produced a parson from its native population while I have been here — no great surprise, perhaps, when people have ever before them the memory of the visit by the theological college. But that is unfair: many of the locals have said since how much they gained from the experience — though I suspect distance lends enchantment — and some correspond regularly even now. When I talk about the village not having produced a clergyman, I mean that no one has ever emerged from an adult confirmation class or a Lent group, or indeed from any of our regular services, to offer himself for the ordained ministry. Statistically this is not surprising since, from its ten thousand parishes, the Church of England produces only about four hundred new clergy each year. I suppose that means we can expect a vocation in Marton every twenty-five years.

I have often tried to work out the reasons for this slow turnover. Pay and conditions are quite good even in an age when glebe land has been commandeered by the bureaucracy in Church House. And there is a legitimate sense in which one can speak of the clergyman's status. He is, after all, self-employed — though there has been more than one story about parsons mischievously writing, under 'Employer' on the tax form, 'The Father Almighty', 'Higher Authority' and so on. The parson was working 'flexi-hours' before anyone else, and if that means that some of his evenings are taken up with parish meetings and fund-raising activities, it also accounts for the fact that you can often see more parsons than ice-cream men on a hot day at the Test Match.

The old jibe claims the parson has reversed the Fourth Commandment to declare 'One day shalt thou labour and do all thy work and on the other six thou shalt take it easy'. And some ancient or mythical parishioner is supposed to have said, 'O aye, God is like the parson — you never see him during the week and you can't understand him on Sunday.'

Even in secularized England the parson still receives much respect. Who else but the vicar is immediately welcomed into every house in the land excepting those belonging to a handful of militant atheists who fear indoctrination? The parson is, as it were, preferred when it comes to the small courtesies of life in the shops or in the pub; he is asked to 'do things' and to 'open functions', and in many of life's activities he is the most obvious choice to say those 'few words' that make the social wheels run smoothly. He is not so much excused his eccentricities as expected to parade them now and again for the amusement of the general population. The expectation that the parson shall move freely between the religious and secular realms is part of the genius of English Christianity. He is called to be a Holy Fool and sometimes to be simply a fool. If he does not see this he is merely unctuous; and unctuousness in the clergy is despised.

I preach about ordination once a year in Marton, usually in Lent when spiritual exercises are taken to with a little more gusto than usual. I occasionally let drop the idea of vocation in our discussion groups and there is a general parley about what is meant by 'going into the Church'. Mrs Crawford, the sacristan, who would have been ordained a quarter of a century ago if the church had consented to overlook her gender, once replied stormily to the debate: ' "Going into the Church"? What's all this talk about going into the Church? I go into the church twice a week to put out fresh vestments and replenish the wine and water. We all went into the church at our baptism. When the Vicar talks about "going into the Church" he means discovering a vocation to the sacred ministry — if he doesn't mind my saying so.' Her brows knitting as she looked up from the other knitting in her lap, you felt that it mattered little whether you minded her saying so or not. It is one of Mrs Crawford's pet expressions, a sort of trade mark. There is another expression which she frequently comes out with as a kind of postscript to her disdain: 'Well now, I've said my piece.'

A couple of years ago, on Mothering Sunday, I noticed a stranger in the congregation — a tall man, aged about thirty. He took his place right at the front and joined in the service vigorously, standing straight-backed for the hymns and the Creed, following the prayers with quiet but obvious devotion, following also, as I discovered later, the readings from the Old and New Testaments in his own copy of the Hebrew and Greek originals. He seemed shy and he politely resisted all invitations to join the rest of the congregation for coffee after the service. His exaggerated posture and hearty singing (not always in agreement as to pitch and intonation with other folks' rendering of Hymns A. & M. Revised) caught the attention of the choirboys who christened him 'Holy Joe'.

A few weeks after Easter the stranger stayed at his devotions for a long time after the service had finished. As I passed by his pew on my way out he stood up and said, 'Father, may I introduce myself?' He spoke in a deep, resonant voice — the sort of voice you would expect Abraham to speak in. And scarcely anyone ever referred to the clergy as 'Father' in these parts. Duffield came to the end of his voluntary and shuffled out through the back vestry. I was alone with the devout and scholarly stranger. 'Christopher Boyd-Martin, Father.' He gave my hand a potent grip.

'Come across to the vicarage, won't you?'

'I'm afraid I can't. Not now.' He looked at his feet and fingered the gold edging on the leaves of his Testament. Then he looked up towards the west window, as if for inspiration. 'I must go and prepare lunch for my mother. We live in York. But I would like to talk with you, urgently. Would after Evensong be a good time?'

As soon as I had said that would be fine, he smiled briefly, offered his hand again, then strode off. He seemed to cover the distance from the chancel to the font in no more than three paces.

When I arrived in church at six o'clock, Mr Boyd-Martin was already at his prayers. He remained kneeling until the first hymn. Throughout the service he maintained his usual scrupulous piety but during the sermon he shuffled in his seat and looked agitated, preoccupied. Later, in my study, he was quite calm again as he told me his life story.

'After Cambridge I went into the Civil Service — as a translator. I enjoyed that a lot. Anyhow, I had a bad patch with regard to my health. But I'm fine now. Since my father died, I've looked after my mother. She's a cripple.' It turned out that he now worked in the reference library at the university but that he did not enjoy this as much as the Foreign Office. He would not take a glass of sherry — he never drank. As we talked he glanced up at my bookshelves and the look on his face seemed to suggest that he had noted all the titles and found nothing of particular interest. 'Father, I will come to the point. I hope you can help me. You see I want to offer myself for the priesthood.' His speech had become anxious, imploring, almost prayerful.

'Well, I am delighted to hear it.' My next question was embarrassing. 'What made you — how can I put it? — what made you come to Marton, to me rather than go to your own vicar?'

'You will think me an awful church-taster but I stopped going to our local church — that's St Agnes — when the new vicar came. I'm afraid the service is not what I've been used to. Guitars, choruses, dancing in the chancel — well, that wasn't the way I was brought up.'

My mind went back to the college visit. 'No, well, we don't have much of that in Marton.'

It was a long and at times an uncomfortable discussion. Boyd-Martin seemed, for all his enthusiasm, to be keeping something back. I was waiting for what I felt would be the sudden revelation that would account for his nervousness. He could not sit still. He would drum on the chair arm for a few seconds, then he would check himself, cross and uncross his legs, take out his pen and fidget with the screw mechanism. A March gale was getting up and the old vicarage itself seemed to creak nervously.

Suddenly he thrust his hands on to his knees as if in performance of some physical exercise. He looked straight ahead. It was dark outside and I became aware that I could see two Boyd-Martins: the stiff fellow on the edge of the armchair and his equally stiff reflection looking through the window from among the tombstones and crosses in the graveyard opposite. 'The trouble is, Father, that I am not worthy of the priesthood'. He said this with vehemence, almost with contrition.

I shrugged. 'The unworthiness of the priest does not invalidate his ministry — that's what the Prayer Book says. Else heaven help the lot of us, so to speak.'

At once there was much more spirit in his conversation. 'Oh, I know that we're all unworthy in a general sort of way; but I am particularly unworthy.'

'That was St Paul's failing too, wasn't it — pride! Not content to be an ordinary sinner. He had to be the Chief of Sinners.'

'Ah, but in my case it's all true!'

'It always is. And what's so special about your sins then? Have you murdered someone or something?'

For a moment I imagined he looked almost disappointed that he was unable to count this crime among his misdoings. Once the conversation had turned to sin, I could tell he felt on more secure ground. He did not exactly make a formal confession though I guessed that, given his High Church instincts, he would need little encouragement to do so. In my experience, most of the confusing problems to afflict the soul come not so much from the lofty world of doctrine and metaphysical theology as from what might happen to be going wrong at present in our daily routine. It was not hard to understand that a sensitive intelligent man like Boyd-Martin, hemmed in between his invalid mother and the recesses of the reference library, should feel the need to pour out his thoughts to a sympathetic audience. Who better than a priest in a church whose worship turned out to be convivial, and which had the convenient remoteness of being set in the next parish but one? I threw another log on the fire and it blazed briefly, brightly. Boyd-Martin said, 'But I am serious about the priesthood. And I have no illusions. My uncle was a priest and so I know what the job entails in the way of tedium and routine — and disappointments.'

'Well then, we must put the wheels in motion for you to try your vocation. I will write to the Bishop about you — and, of course, I shall have to get in touch with your parish priest to let him know what's going on. Perhaps you might call and see him yourself.'

'Perhaps.'

There was a very loud silence. I walked over to the desk to get pen and paper. 'Now then, I must take down a few details. Christopher Boyd-Martin, right? Date of birth, Christopher?'

He went and stood with his back to the window. 'Why d'you want to know that?'

'Just administration, you know. Name. Address. Date of Birth. The diocesan office will have to have something to recognise your file by.'

He was almost in tears. He would not say what was the matter. I tried the light-hearted approach: 'There's nothing to worry about. You did say you hadn't actually committed a murder didn't you? Well, the office will need some way of referring to you — I mean, so far as they're concerned you might be St Peter himself.'

'I am!'

'You are St . . .! I swallowed my sentence when I realized he was not joking. His face took on a studied transcendental aspect and his speech became very calm.

'I am St Peter. The Lord has sent me to root out error and immorality in the Church . . .' He put his hand into his jacket pocket. I half expected him to withdraw a bunch of golden keys '. . . and I must go now and report to the Lord all I have seen in Marton.'

He was courteous but insistent and so eventually I accompanied him to his car and he drove off immaculately towards York.

I returned to the study at once and telephoned his vicar. He did not sound at all surprised. 'Yes, Peter, I knew he had been visiting you at Marton. I wondered how long it would be before he came to see you. He does the same thing wherever he goes apparently, poor soul. I know his psychiatrist. There's no cause for alarm. The psychiatrist says he's a mild schizophrenic. No danger to himself or anyone else. His delusions are confined entirely to this Church thing. He copes wonderfully at work — and with his mother. Look, I'll let things ride for a couple of days, then I'll call round and see him.'

I never saw Christopher Boyd-Martin again — and Marton is still waiting for its first candidate for Holy Orders.

8

THERE WERE GIANTS IN THOSE DAYS

Life mimics Art, or so they say. I had never grasped the full significance of this saying until a real parson with the habits and style of a stage parson came to serve in our rural deanery. For the duration of his brief incumbency, clergy meetings were unbearable.

The Reverend Murdoch A. Spry (the 'A' stood for Athelstan) arrived at St James', Barton — the next village but one — on a clear icy day in January. Even the manner of his coming had an occult flavour about it. One Charles Tomlinson was appointed to be the new vicar of St James' but he withdrew at the last minute and within three weeks we were joined by Mr Spry. He might have been named Mr Smile, for his large face was set perpetually on full beam. The Rural Dean once drew me on one side after Chapter Meeting and said, 'D'you think it's the cast of his jaw or something? I mean, he never lets up. Every time you look at him, there he is grinning back as if he'd just doubled the freewill offering scheme. Makes you wonder how he deals with funerals.'

Murdoch's voice was not simply parsonical; it was deafening. And his presence was so overwhelming — he must have stood six cubits and a span — that when he was nearby you felt you were forcibly being done good to. Someone must once have told him that since he was so tall he ought to stoop slightly, so that those enjoying the pleasure of his company might behold his face as well as hearken to his voice. The super-real personality of the Rev. Spry, whose vocabulary knew not the word 'subtlety', interpreted this as an injunction to take a nose-dive — the nose being one aspect of his physiology where he lacked nothing — on to anyone who stood less than five feet ten. So you learned to look out for him at parish bun-fights where he would loom up like an iceberg in the mist and sink anyone nearby with one swift nod of that huge dome. To add to his general incongruity he could, throughout these genial and accidental assaults, be seen to be curling his finger around his china teacup like a picture of elegance.

In fact his accidentalism was unconscious. The whole spectacle of beaming ungainliness was all unawares. That was the most infuriating part about it, for it meant there was no prospect of correction. The sudden rush of his sedentary bulk smashed six chairs during his first four weeks in the parish. The subsequent apology for damage done lost nothing in sincerity for being so often made; in fact the enormous clergyman soon earned a reputation for being sincere. As Mrs Dovedale at 'The Grange' said, 'When Mr Spry asks you how you are, you know he really means it.' It was on account of one of Spry's pilgrimages of sincerity that Mrs Dovedale was not at all well — having her left arm in plaster at the age of eighty-three. Spry had learned from Dr Edge that the old girl was having rather more trouble than usual with her failing heart. Quick as an earthquake he had heaved himself round to offer condolence and a nice line in loud afternoon chat. Seeking refuge from the dipping brow and the decibels, Mrs Dovedale had backed away from her visitor on the pretext of fetching from the top of the cellar stairs a bottle of her famous ginger wine. Overcome perhaps by the surreality of events, she had missed her footing and overbalanced. She coped remarkably with the accident itself and with Spry's attempts at first aid. From her bed in York District Hospital she said to the Rural Dean: 'I know he means well but I don't think I'm fit enough to take any more of his sick visiting for the time being.'

Murdoch Spry was also, as the psychologists say, 'disorientated as to time and place'. Although he had a reputation for scholarship, and he could pin-point historical events with minute accuracy centuries ago in the time of such as Amenhotep IV or Augustus Caesar, he never seemed sure whether it was Tuesday or Thursday in his own parish. This made for interesting variations in the times of services, as evidenced by crusty Bert Mackay who lived right opposite St James's, and noticed Spry one morning standing in all his vestments on the pavement by the west door.

'What are you doin' Mr Spry — special service or summat?'

'Maybe we'll get you to church one of these Sundays, Mr Mackay,' came the riposte quick as a flash.

'Appen you will an' all. But I'm blowed if I'm a-practisin' for it on a Wednesday.'

According to Mackay, poor Murdoch looked dazed for a minute, then ducked sharply back into church only to emerge sheepishly, though still smiling, twenty minutes later. 'Morning again Mr Mackay! I can't think what I was thinking of.'

Murdoch went in for what you might call 'creative liturgy'. Every chapter meeting began with a celebration of the Holy Communion in one of the local churches. When it was the turn of St James's, I telephoned Murdoch the night before to remind him he should expect us. After I had put the phone down I felt I had behaved in a rather patronizing fashion, for Murdoch had bawled courteously into my ear that of course he knew we were coming and that he had, as a matter of preparation, got Mrs Beasley to make one of her special cakes for us. Surely we exaggerated Murdoch's eccentricity? Surely his amnesia was only partial and intermittent? I was annoyed with myself for thinking the worst and I tried to picture some means of making amends. Perhaps I could take him a packet of that fine china tea which Barbara had brought from the delicatessen.

The day of the chapter happened to be the Annunciation of the Blessed Virgin Mary, Lady Day, the 25th of March. It was a fine spring morning, the air crisp, the hedgerows beginning to look hazy with their early colours. The proper liturgical colour for the Annunciation is, of course, white and, sure enough, the altar at the lovely medieval church of St James's was draped in its best white frontal with a golden cross on the front. We shuffled into the front pew to wait for Murdoch to come out of the vestry and lead the service. I felt even more chastened for my dark thoughts about his forgetfulness when I noticed from the quiet purring of the fans that he had remembered to turn on the heating.

Suddenly there came a crash from the vestry followed by a silence during which the Rural Dean looked up from his prayer book and gave me an ominous stare. Then Murdoch emerged in his *red* vestments. He seemed to cover the ground between the vestry and the altar without any need for the passage of time. He stood in the sanctuary, red against white like a liturgical Wars of the Roses. Arms raised, face beaming at the congregation of his fellow clergy, he looked like the Demon King. There followed the Collect, Epistle and Gospel not for the Annunciation, but for the Ascension, a maladjustment which he seemed to have an inkling of half-way through the service, for his voice dropped to an unprecedented quietness and his matching red face grew even redder. But there was a superfluity of all that is unexpected with Murdoch, and among his vagaries he possessed virtuosity: after the Gospel he gave a short but penetrating homily on 'the means of grace'.

There was the occasion when, at the municipal crematorium, he first forgot and then remembered to ask the undertaker for the death certificate. 'A right do', said Michael Derrington. 'You should have seen him charging down the aisle after the words of committal and shouting "Do I want a green ticket?" Well, I could have soon told him the answer to that one.' There were the innumerable occasions when he locked himself out of his house and was only rescued by the petite and long-suffering Mrs Beasley who climbed through the window and let him in. I only found out about these goings-on when one evening at the Deanery Synod he thrust his illuminated visage in my direction and asked loudly where he could get a pair of lisle stockings. Members of Synod seemed to hold me in a new regard ever after that. Then there was the unseemly incident after he reckoned he had reserved seats for St James' Mothers' Union at a performance of *Salad Days*, but they discovered that they were actually booked in to *Confessions of a Teenage Sex Fiend..*

Throughout these minor (and not so minor) catastrophes, his smile was not dimmed nor his good humour abated. Though a few who seemed to have been singled out for an excess of his bumbling attention learned to flee at the sight of him, he was generally held in the highest esteem by his parishioners and particularly well loved by the young people. It might have been possible to turn a deaf ear to his loud mouth for ever, to bear with equanimity the noise of crumbling furniture and even to grow accustomed to his radical sense of timekeeping. In other words, The Reverend Murdoch Athelstan Spry, with his reputation for cheerful eccentricity, might have settled in Barton for half a generation — had not there developed the unfortunate saga after he fell in love with Louise Treddle, spinster of that parish.

Miss Treddle was well-known as a lady of deep religious sensitivities but any temptation towards spiritual abstraction was tempered by her even more well-known concern for the material welfare of the parochial clergy. She lived alone in Barton Lodge, having lost her parents in an accident on the motorway in France. Had she lived in the days of Jane Austen, she might perhaps have been occupied as a governess at one of the finer houses, for she was a woman of many accomplishments, including painting and musicianship. She was the youngest person ever to become headmistress at the village school. It was this occupation which provided her with the opportunity for showing kindness to the clergy. Murdoch's predecessor, also a bachelor, was invited to the school every Friday morning to lead the assembly and to teach Religious Knowledge to the Upper Juniors. Miss Treddle took it upon herself to reward the parson for this otherwise unpaid work, providing him weekly with home-made bread and cakes, an act of charity which was continued during Murdoch's incumbency.

After his first visit to the school when he forgot to take home his cakes, a girl and a boy from Miss Treddle's own class ran round to his house with them and with a note from their teacher inviting the Vicar for tea at the Lodge the following day. That day was a day of black clouds and horizontal rain as Murdoch in his galoshes and cape struggled along the empty village street in search of the Lodge. Miss Treddle was carefully placing a silver tray on the low table before the fire when the dogs began to bark and, looking up, she saw the drenched Vicar wrestling with the catch on the garden gate. She noticed how he smiled even under adversity. Armed with an umbrella and followed by the inquisitive dogs she ran to let him in.

'I'm so glad you could come. You mustn't mind the dogs.' Murdoch took a steel comb to his saturated baldness and peered through his misty spectacles at Miss Treddle's paintings in the hall.

'Ah! a real artist. How delightful to have one's own work hanging in one's own hall.' He knew how to frame a compliment but he barked his words so loudly that the startled dogs ran off towards the kitchen.

They sat for a long time before the rosy fire sipping their tea and sampling Miss Treddle's cakes. They talked about the school, of course, but also about painting. Murdoch, though he might stumble on his course through the tangible world, was not lost in the world of the Great Masters. Even as they talked late into the afternoon, as the glow of the fire cast spiky shadows into the corners of the room and the light from the window fell onto Louise's face, he thought how she looked like a Vermeer. He reached for more cake but the silver tray was empty of food except for the sugar lumps, so he ate one of them instead. Miss Treddle was so delighted with his conversation that she hardly noticed the way he surged back and forth in his chair, crossing and uncrossing his feet so vigorously that all the ornaments in the hearth were set in perpetual vibration.

It was a scene often to be re-enacted in the months that followed. Not every Saturday was wet, and twice in October they were able to sit out on the garden seat and watch the leaves gather on the grass like scorched paper. Sometimes they walked through the village together as far as Croft's farm where Miss Treddle bought fresh eggs. Once, they put on scarves and woolly hats and set off in the other direction through the copse and up past the disused cottages to the windmill. The villagers watched fascinated and waited for the announcement that the young headmistress and the tall vicar were to become engaged. Meanwhile, Miss Treddle and the Reverend Spry — or Louise and Murdoch as they had begun to call each other — were much enriched by their mutual affection. Barton had never seemed such an idyllic setting for Miss Treddle's work. Her paintings became brighter, the colours more generous, the lines bolder. Even the schoolchildren became more amenable and on Friday mornings Susan Templeton, the pubescent register monitor, all long blonde hair and knowing glances, would smile coyly at her headmistress and inquire through her lisp whether Mr Spry was coming to school today. Miss Treddle herself smiled more frequently, seemed to develop a more assured touch in her dealings with the staff and generally appeared full of energy and optimism as she visited the classroom.

Murdoch also seemed more carefree as he went about doing good. It was even said that he no longer shouted quite so loudly, which must have been good news for the sick and the frail on his visiting list. Sermons, too, were less pre-occupied with the sins, negligencies and ignorances of old Adam and more concerned with the boundless love and mercy of Our Heavenly Father. Moreover, there was a gradual increase in extra-biblical material in his sermonizing and it was after a wonderfully unexpurgated meditation on the relationship of Abelard and Héloïse that Mrs Drury, (organist at St James's) squinting furtively under her triangular cap, was drawn to say, 'I reckon there'll be a lady about the vicarage before Rogationtide!'

And so it might have been were it not for the scandal occasioned by Murdoch's incorrigible inappropriateness. I mean, if an absent-minded vicar, oblivious of times and seasons, insistent in his confusion of day with night, arrives now and again on the doorstep of the blacksmith or even of the postmaster at an hour strange for visitors, people merely giggle behind their hands and by their tittle-tattle increase his lovable eccentricity; but if any man in a village, and particularly a clergyman, falls into the habit of paying nocturnal visits to an unmarried woman who happens also to be the seamstress of the children's moral education, then the upright villagers will find it hard not to be outraged. And so in the Post Office one Monday morning in that hard frozen January, Mrs Spargeon complained, 'I heard this

clomping along the street at past one in the morning — I'm
always awake then because I have to get Charlie his sleeping
tablet — we daren't keep them by the side of the bed since
he almost swallowed the lot in his stupor — and I looked
out and saw Mr Spry. Well, he went right across the road to
the Lodge and hammered on door. Of course, you can see
right into Miss Treddle's from our front bedroom — and she
doesn't always pull the curtains. Anyhow, her light goes on
and she gets out of bed and goes downstairs in her dressing-
gown to let him in. 'Course, I'm not saying as she meant any
wrong like, *but . . .*'

No one who knew Murdoch held the slightest suspicion
of impropriety, but it was obviously and urgently necessary
that someone should have a word in his ear before an even
more unexpurgated, though ill-founded, rumour of the
Abelard and Héloïse genre gained currency in the village.
When the Rural Dean took him quietly on one side after a
routine Chapter Meeting and suggested to him that he
observe the usual nine o'clock curfew on visitations,
Murdoch merely looked flabbergasted. When he recovered
and the smile returned to his face, he expostulated in his
usual loud voice that he had not intended any mischief. At
this sudden bawling of the word 'mischief' and of other
words that followed it, such as 'had no idea', 'middle of the
night' and 'interference', it was difficult for the rest of the
Chapter to pretend they were out of earshot. I am afraid
that some of the brethren glanced across to where Murdoch
was waving his arms about behind the glass partition and
were seen to laugh. Innocent Murdoch was riled and he
stormed out without another word. Unfortunately, his
righteous indignation did not encourage him to greater
circumspection and that same night he paid another of his
after-hours calls to Miss Treddle who on this occasion was
sleeping so soundly that the affronted clergyman was heard

hammering at her door for a full five minutes until, as the ever-watchful Mrs Spargeon reported, 'she came down in her nightdress and let him in.'

The reverberations would have scored eleven on the Richter Scale. The vicar was even more stared at in the street and Cathy Middleton in Class III embarrassed the whole assembly one morning by calling out, 'Are you in love with Miss Treddle, sir?' An awkward silence fell upon the shops when Louise appeared. A few parents were heard talking in 'The Acorn', wondering whether they should withdraw their children from the school. As I went into the offices of *the Advertiser* to publicize our Shrove Tuesday Dance, I gained the impression that the lads in the news room, bored to insanity by endless flower shows and W.I. open evenings, were dangling their fingers expectantly over the typewriter keys, awaiting the one piece of hard news that would allow them to begin the item, 'My Love for Vicar by Village Headmistress'.

As soon as the rumours reached as far as the diocesan authorities, the Bishop acted swiftly by summoning Murdoch and inquiring whether he would like to take responsibility for the Sisters of Divine Compassion near Flamborough. It was a compassionate move on the Bishop's part: 'The chaplaincy is combined with a small parish. You would, of course, live in the vicarage and visit the convent every day. No one', he cleared his throat, 'is suggesting that you take a vow of celibacy or anything like that!'

And so the enormous clergyman departed, and St James' Barton were faced with a long and difficult interregnum as recompense for all their chattering. In the circumstances they were fortunate, and managed to entice a young married vicar with four children to occupy the parsonage and restore order among them. Miss Treddle waited a while before concluding that her own happiness might be best served by a move to another school. A suitable vacancy arose in the village of Stansley on the North Yorkshire moors, eight miles from Flamborough.

They were married in September, the Bishop himself officiating, Murdoch beaming more brightly than ever, his 'I will' resounding above the noise of the wind, Louise pretty as one of Degas' dancers at his side. The wedding cake was presented by the Sisters of Divine Compassion.

9

THE NEW BABEL

The latest piece of zapping-up contrived by our ecclesiastical superiors to interfere with a decent morning's head-scratching over our intellectual vocation was an Archdeaconry Conference on 'Communication: Mission: Evangelism'. The first intimation of this new project came in a plain brown envelope and was headed with a picture, a line drawing of what looked like the Holy Spirit as a dove nosediving behind a copy of the *Daily Telegraph*. Beneath it were the words 'Communicate! Evangelize! Grow!' The whole page was simply zapping with exclamation marks and underlinings and with the word 'YOU' so frequently inscribed in capital letters that you wondered if the Diocesan Office had been taken over by Lord Kitchener. The gist of the encyclical was that the ancient threefold order of ministry, bishops, priests and deacons, could do with a refresher course on the art of communication. Except on this prospectus it was seen not so much as an art as a science. At least there were traces of a kind of scientific vocabulary but unfortunately it increased rather than dissipated the mystery of how anything is communicated at all. We were not more or less good at talking but 'possessed skills of verbalization'; our sermons should be neither believable nor unbelievable but 'display a high credibility profile'; in case we imagined that our job should involve us in merely talking to our parishioners, we were to be reassured by 'interpersonal skills and group dynamics evaluations'; we do not simply 'tell' but 'disseminate information'; neither should we expect our parishioners — who no longer dwell in parishes but in 'pastoral situations' — to 'read, mark, learn and inwardly digest' but to 'amplify techniques for the accommodation and assimilation of appropriate data', instead.

The atmosphere of excitement which surrounded all these gimmicks — or I should perhaps say 'strategies for dialogue' — gathered around a fine eighteenth century house on the edge — or I should perhaps say 'located on the edge' — of the Yorkshire Dales. I heaved myself, with my colleague the vicar of Trentham, through the early morning mist towards the conference centre and I could not help wondering what the Brontë sisters would have made of this dialectical incursion into their territory. The mist still had not lifted by the time of our arrival. It was silent, still and damp. The old house and the woods in the distance looked as if they were hiding behind net curtains. As we went in we were met by the smell of breakfast. In the large morning room, clergy stood about in small groups sipping their coffee and exchanging ecclesiastical gossip in that earnest pressed humour style which parsons adopt *en masse*, and which is as much like an advertisement for insincerity as anything you will find outside the Houses of Parliament. I do not say it *is* insincerity, only that it is like insincerity. It is, as it were, a general habit, the odium of the trade. The 'Good Mornings!' rang out in artificially high-pitched tone, there were extravagant shakings of hands, laughter both stylized and loud and much chin-stroking reminiscence of such as 'Old so-and-so who used to have Bagley, Sendall and Upper Creepy-in-the-Forest'.

This refined flea market was interrupted by a jolly fellow with a ginger beard and a bald pate who leapt on to the rostrum waving a bunch of papers and inquired whether 'gentlemen would mind assembling in two minutes when I shall endeavour to tell you where to go.' There was huge laughter at this witticism and a procession of dog-collars began to shuffle its way to the hatch in order to replace teacups and plates of biscuits. The man with the ginger beard gingered us up with trailers for the day's activities. We would first of all be welcomed by the Bishop — actually the Bishop had welcomed many of us already as he darted among the crowd like a piece of purple flotsam on a grey/black sea — who would lead us in prayer; then we would be addressed by the Diocesan Communications Officer; after lunch we were to 'break up into our groups'.

When the Bishop had prayed for 'all whose vocation and business lies in the media' — an unfortunate sequence of words — we sang the hymn freshly composed for our Conference and printed on the inside back cover of the 'Diocesan Communications Pack':

'Inspire, we pray, imagination
Help us in communication
So that men shall ne'er refuse
To listen to the gospel news.'

'And now', said the Bishop, 'We are all in Rob's hands'.
'Whose hands?' asked my friend from Trentham.
'Rob's', I whispered.
'Oh, that's news,' he smirked, 'I thought he said "God's hands".'

Robert — 'call me Rob' — Jenkins began in lively style with a few jokes of 'the chorus girl said to the Bishop' variety suitably laundered for the episcopal presence and remythologized to include a 'communications slant'. Then the room was darkened and we were shown an extract from an old Monty Python film: *The Dead Parrot Sketch*. This was, said the ebullient Rob, 'an exercise in profound non-communication at a deep level'. As soon as the lights went out, I noticed that John Eddlestone from Trentham had lapsed into a sleep situation.

The film finished. The Communications Officer then

experienced a minor communications difficulty as he tried by speech and gesture to get the hard-of-hearing attendant to draw back the curtains. At last he succeeded and the room was pierced with bright sunshine and the Communications Officer's features were rendered invisible against the background of the large picture window. The sunlight startled Eddlestone and he snuffled and snorted his way back to consciousness.

'When I was in the States,' said Rob with the easy familiarity of the globetrotter, 'I really had my peepers busted wide open on this communications pitch.' He spoke in the avid mid-Atlantic accent adopted by television personalities on late-night chat shows. 'Sure, I always thought I was coming across loud and clear. None of my congregation ever seemed to fall asleep on me but . . .' Abruptly the soporific monologue cleared and the speaker began to smack a square of aluminium as hard as he could. Eddlestone, who had already begun to sink back into the mists of forgetfulness, lurched forward, his hand on his heart, his heart in his mouth. From the expressions on the faces of many other clergy, it was hard to tell whether they had interpreted the sudden din as a raucous overture to the Last Trump or merely the gong sounding for lunch.

'See! See!' chortled the silhouette (when he must have meant 'Hear! Hear!') 'You had assumed an Overt Listening Posture but you weren't really listening. It needed the stimulus of this little fellow' — he shook his silver square gently and it shimmered in the sun — 'to rouse you into a True Listening State'. He went over to a blackboard and chalked something. An old parson a dozen rows back stood up, his hand shielding his eyes, and said, 'Could someone draw that curtain please? We can't see what the Communications Officer is writing.' Someone adjusted the curtain, or at least half-adjusted it so that the stage was now divided into one section that looked like a funeral parlour, all black drapes and dusty sunbeams, while the other section was just as dazzling as before.

Rob Jenkins had written only the initials OLP and TLP. 'Now', he said, 'I guess that most of your congregation is usually in this state — Overt Listening Posture . . .' He underlined the initials with his aluminium-free hand. 'But your job is to make sure they attain this.' He knocked with his knuckles over TLP. 'Problem: how to achieve this situation?' The problem turned out to be a rhetorical question. 'We realise the TLP of our audience with the aid of this little fellow, the Auditory Stimulus.' He waggled the aluminium. 'Now you good people weren't expecting me to produce this little fellow, so that means he is an Unconditioned Stimulus you see. And the Unconditioned Stimulus' — he shook the thing again and grinned — 'produced in you an Unconditioned Response. That means no one told you in advance you should prepare yourselves to be startled.' Suddenly he laughed and his mouth gaped in a huge banana-split smile. A few strokes of his beard and he recovered himself. 'But now, you see, the Unconditioned Stimulus applied to your OLP has produced TLP as an Unconditioned Response, as a behavioural result of the Unconditioned Stimulus and, if I hammer it again' — he did so and the brethren narrowed their eyes and held their hands to their ears — 'it produces in you this time a Conditioned Response.' He rushed across to the blackboard and scowled as he quickly erased his earlier lesson. Then he scrawled — carefully, almost mystically, as if he were a reincarnation of Dr Mesmer — the formula:

'OLP + UCS = UCR (TLP)
TLP + CS = CR (TLP2)

'Where', he added quietly, as if his explanation were

unnecessary, 'TLP2 means simply TLP on a continuing basis.' He stood with his arms elevated like a priest before the altar. His placid smile seemed to pronounce QED. The parsons sat about like stunned flies. But Rob the Communicator had not finished yet. 'So you see', he spoke more quickly, like a telephone caller trying to get in as many words as possible before the pips. But it would have been a very expensive call. 'I've been teaching you some psychology so that you can really get into what motivates your audience – what turns them on . . .'

'I wish someone would turn him off,' said the newly roused Eddlestone. 'He's a voice like Bob Hope and a subject like the Book of Leviticus.' He was quickly shushed by an enthusiastic clergyman on the row in front.

'Methodological considerations,' considered rambling Rob, 'are not everything. The trick is to find something which will do the same job in your pulpits as this little fellow here'. He banged the Conditioned Stimulus on his knee. 'OK now, I'll take questions.'

The only questions came from a parson in the front row who, as he told us, was 'a keen student of psychological techniques and indeed of the whole requirement to foster interdisciplinary awareness'. Rob nodded vigorously. These were not questions as such, but miniature lectures on their own, as if the questioner were trying to repay the Communications Officer in kind. It was like a tennis match between the two of them over the heads of the rest of the assembly.

'Must all CRs be based ultimately on UCRs?'

A fast backhand from Rob: 'Yea. Via the UCs.'

The unexpected lob: 'But what independently variable factors determine which Ss are ultimately UCs?'

The smash: 'The Variables themselves.' Game, set and match.

After this the Bishop tried to ask a question but it was

clear he was out of his depth. Something about Freud and
the unconscious mind. Rob regarded the naïve question
benignly as any parson in the room would regard the child's
conundrum 'Who made God?' Then we were asked to go to
our groups and discuss the fixed questions until lunchtime.
Our group met in a back room which featured an old piano
and was scattered about with rather worn sports equipment.
Half a dozen old sports sat down on the ricketty chairs and
began to rummage around in their brainboxes for some sort
of response to the high-powered promptings of the morning.
One old boy with a curved pipe said, 'The Master of my
college always told us to gesture *before* the word you want
them to hear, not afterwards.' Another said, 'Our Principal
reckoned a sermon should be "about God and about five
minutes".' Chuckles.

A wiry curate with steel-framed spectacles took many
words to say that he did not think what we *said* was very
important, but the quality of our lives was. After this vaguely
methodistical interpolation the conversation settled upon
the usual subjects of clergy meetings: 'Are you still where
you were, George? How long have you been there now?'
'Do you get much trouble from the new Archdeacon? I've
heard he's a bit of a martinet.'

There were other burning issues, among them fabric
funds, funeral fees and the diocesan quota. But the steel-
framed curate was anxious to return us to our proper subject
— a tiresome prospect for the brethren who were just
warming up to a nice fit of indignation about the poor rate
paid by the diocese for car mileage expenses on local
committee business. The curate turned out to be neither so
methodistical nor so pietistic as at first feared. He marched
across to the window and lit a cigarette: 'Gimmicks. Jargon.
Behavioural psychology. Does he think Our Lord used these
tricks in the Sermon on the Mount? "Blessed are the

psychologists for they shall be psychoanalyzed . . ." ' There was, between an anecdote about the diocesan architect and some generalized condemnation of central policy on church-yards, more of this irreverent banter until the gong sounded for lunch. It reminded me of the wordy communications man and his square of aluminium.

After lunch followed the most indigestible part of the conference. Back we sauntered into the hot bright morning room now filled with the whiff of cigars and strong coffee. The brethren, having eaten well, were in a fine mood to be lulled by talk into a state of blissful reverie. Clearly this had been anticipated by the organizers. Up jumped effervescent Rob, minus aluminium, to tell us, 'The afternoon belongs to YOU!' His long preamble amounted to the announcement that we were all going to have to move about a bit. 'Communication can be non-verbal as well as verbal, tactile as well as oral. It can belong as much to the physical and somatic modes as to the literary mode.' We were going to be asked to touch one another in the interests of science. And more than touch: 'To communicate our trust (as Christians) we are going to run across the room towards our partners and cast ourselves into their care — trusting they will hold us and support us.'

So began a dyspepsic pageant in which embarrassed clergymen leaned forwards (or backwards) into the arms of partners, trusting the body of flesh to the arms of others. It was like the resurrection of the recalcitrant dead and accompanied by much perspiration and grunting, Rob's voice over all constantly cajoling, exhorting and summing-up: 'You see, if you wanna communicate, you first gotta establish a two-way trust mechanism!' The presence of deaconesses and other lady workers gave to the proceedings a mildly sensual feel — in a dessicated sort of way. My mind went back to all those Sunday School parties of my childhood that were organised by stout evangelical ladies and largely consisted in such sub-libidinous procedures as passing oranges between knees or winding long threads of cotton through your neighbour's party clothes. Perhaps they could have done with the ministrations of our present-day communicating psychologists.

At half-past three Eddlestone, speeding from the clutches of the robust Miss Aldicene Merryweather, asked how long it was to plenary session and dismiss. Not long. At four o'clock we all gathered to hear the group reports, some of which were much more copious and learned than our own, and to hear the Bishop say how grateful we all were to the expert Rob. He was sure we would all go back to our parishes filled with a new zeal to communicate with our people who were surely in for an exciting time as a result of, etc. etc. . . .

As we went out into the world we had to pass our mentor who stood by a display of books and pamphlets on the subject dearest to his heart. Warm as it was he wore a raincoat and a red and blue university scarf hung loosely about his neck. He had a firm grip and piercing eye. He was only too willing to come to any of our parishes and talk to small groups. He wanted to be thought of as a co-ordinating resource person for the whole diocese. And for all I know, some may have thought of him in exactly that way. As we left, Eddlestone turned back and began to cast his eyes once more over the bookstall. Rob noticed him, left off his handshaking for a minute and asked if he could be of any help. Eddlestone looked down into the bearded pedagogue's earnest face. 'Well', he said 'I was just wondering if you had any more of those metal squares. I could do with a draw tin for the coal fire in the vicarage.'

10

OF RIPER YEARS

One Tuesday afternoon last summer I went across to the church to put new candles on the high altar. It was warm, still and unusually bright. The colours of the west window were projected inexactly by the sunlight on to the floor of the chancel so that it seemed you looked at the cool stones through tropical waters. The silence in an empty church always gives me the impression that a hymn has just finished. Just as I was taking down the candlesticks I noticed a man kneeling at the little altar in the side chapel. I took old stubs and new tapers to the vestry where I spent about ten minutes cleaning off embedded wax and making sure the candles were fixed, firm and vertical. As I paused by the lectern I saw that the visitor had finished his prayers and had gone to sit in one of the short pews by the font. I replaced the candles and went to introduce myself. He was a man of about twenty-eight or thirty in a smart dark green suit. He looked anxious, preoccupied, as if he were lost in the middle of an impossible calculation. He spoke first: 'I'm sorry, I hope you don't mind . . .'

'Of course not. We never lock the church. You're welcome.'

'It's just that it's so peaceful. It puts me back together again — you know, to kneel up there for a bit.' He nodded towards the wooden cross on the side altar. The anxious expression was replaced by the blank, meaningless look of someone bored with the effort of polite conversation. His speech was matter-of-fact, monotone.

I said, 'I know. I like to sit in here myself on a summer

afternoon. What is it? —"the still point of the turning world".'

The sun slid behind a cloud and a shadow raced across the wall, then all was still and bright as before. The young man seemed suddenly startled. He began to speak rapidly as if he had run a long distance to deliver an urgent message. 'That's just it. That's what I can't find — stillness. You know, I used to go to church sometimes. Then I stopped and, I don't know, I think I didn't believe anything. I started going again with a friend. He died suddenly. He had a funny valve in his heart and nobody knew. I went to his funeral and all the time I just wanted to shout. I wanted to shout because everybody — the parson, the blokes from the office, even his mother, everybody — they all seemed as if they were just going through the motions — you know, as if nothing were real. And soon Mike would be under the ground and we'd be standing at a bar somewhere drinking and swapping stories about him, and it wouldn't mean anything. I wanted something to happen. I wanted the world to notice — what you said, "the still point"; I wished that time would stop in that graveyard so I could run round to everybody and say, "Look, this is real, see! Mike's dead. This is his funeral. He won't be coming back!" I know it sounds mad but I wanted his death to be marked in some way — not a cross or a gravestone; I don't mean that. I mean some way of telling, some sign that what we were going through — the parson, the undertakers, all the people standing round the grave — well, that it wasn't just ordinary. I picked up a handful of earth. I had this silly feeling that until I threw it on the coffin no one would be able to move. And they'd all just have to stand there — for ever if necessary — but they wouldn't be allowed to move until I said so.'

'Mike — he must have been a very good friend?'

The young man paused. He stood up and thrust his hands deep into his pockets. He was calmer and he began to stroll aimlessly about the baptistry as if he were in a station waiting room. His attention seemed to be fixed on the floor pattern. 'I'd known him from schooldays. He was very religious — always had been. I don't mean ramming it down your throat or anything. But he was the sort of bloke who didn't mind admitting he said his prayers. Church on Sunday, every Sunday, and involved — you know, collecting for charity, discussion groups, the Easter play —.'

'Did you go to church with him?'

He stood still and stared at me as if he was looking for obscure meaning in my question.

'Sometimes. I can't explain it. It didn't mean the same to me as it meant to Mike. I used to watch him during the hymns and prayers. You could tell he really believed it.'

'And you didn't believe it?'

'It was so beautiful. Some of the tunes we used to sing — they'd break your heart. And the church on a summer morning — well, it was like this: warm, bright, full of flowers and everybody in summer clothes. The aroma of the wine at Communion. And afterwards there was a cup of coffee on the grass. Mike knew everybody. Everybody liked him.'

'Did you go up with him to Communion?'

He sat down, his hands still stuffed in his pockets, his lips curling in self-mockery. 'No. I was never confirmed as a boy. Mike told me about the adult classes Mr Barker held — we went to St Giles in Leeds. But I couldn't bring myself to go, not even for Mike. And you're right in what you said, I couldn't believe. The music, the pictures, the fellowship — they were good people — that was something I could appreciate — couldn't do without eventually — but not all the other things. Resurrection. God. Life after death . . .'

As if cued by his words, the church clock began to strike. The young man's voice sounded wearier, more resigned. I felt he was repeating a speech he had made many times to himself. 'I'm a radiographer. I see right to the middle of the human body every day. Sick people. Progressive diseases. Human beings are what? — stuff. Skin, bones, muscles, veins, organs, health, pathology. And we all go the same way. Souls and eternal life and all that — well, that's religion; it's a kind of beautiful comfort that makes life bearable, but in the end —.'

'It doesn't make it bearable for you?'

'It did, in a way, while Mike was alive. I couldn't share his faith, but it didn't matter. I don't know whether I admired him for it or despised him for it. It's a funny thing, he seemed to have enough faith for both of us.'

'And that's why you wanted time to stop when he died?'

'I haven't been to church since — not since he died. There doesn't seem any point.'

'But you came in here!'

'That's different. It's my day off. Just a bit of peace and quiet, that's all.' I looked towards the little altar where he was kneeling when I came in.

He screwed up his eyes and looked at the floor. 'I was desperate. I seemed to have nothing. The whole point of everything had vanished. I don't believe — not in the way people talk about believing. I can't, I've told you, I just can't. But I couldn't stand the emptiness. Have you ever felt emptiness as something heavy? Well, that's what I felt. I thought it would crush me. I knelt at that altar rail and I don't know who or what I was talking to — I mean it's silly to pray if you don't believe — but I kept saying over and over again, "Let there be *something*. Don't let it keep on like this for ever. Please, let there *be* something!" '

'And the vicar came in and disturbed you!'

His eyebrows and lips all wriggled in different directions as if he seemed to smile and wince at the same time. 'No, I didn't mean that. You didn't disturb me. You expect to see vicars in churches.'

'When you're doing your radiography and you come across someone who's ill, d'you believe in the illness or only in its symptoms?'

All at once he looked thoroughly at home. I might have been a stranger in *his* church.

'Well, the symptoms help the doctor diagnose the disease. So in that sense they're only signs, evidence. But then, if you could remove all the symptoms that would mean you'd cured the disease.'

'What about all those signs of religion you mentioned — the music, the pictures, the atmosphere in church, the fellowship — couldn't you see *them* as the symptoms of something?'

'Ah, wait a minute! You can't believe in the signs of religion unless there's something behind them. I mean, if there's no God, then churches and all the trappings are just an illusion, aren't they — wishful thinking?'

'But what if God is not so much, as you say, 'behind' all these . . . symptoms, but *is* them?'

'But there has to be some sort of guarantee, something that decides whether the outward appearances are valid — something that makes religion true . . . or false.'

'I think that is the practice of religion itself.'

'But you can't say that. What if religion isn't really true after all? You can't practise it as if it were true. That would be deluding yourself . . . or hypocrisy.'

'I wonder what a disease is when it has obviously no symptoms? You admit that, in the last resort a disease is its symptoms — because its symptoms are what it actually *does*. If it does nothing at all, then it's hardly a disease.'

'But that's not the way it works with religion!'

'I see. You want a sort of double standard. Ordinary rules of evidence will do for medical science but religion has to

have extra qualifications! What if I were to say, "I don't care
for your talk of symptoms — the high temperature, the
sweating, the thirst, the delirium — show me the fever
behind them"?'

I went behind the altar rail and brushed some fallen petals
off the dust cloth. The young man leaned against the font.

'You and Mike — you obviously thought a lot about each
other. Was that just a symptom?'

'We were friends. It was the real thing. We kept nothing
from each other.'

'And you weren't always asking one another for some
"guarantee" of your friendship *behind* the friendship itself?
Well, we don't make ourselves religious by trying to believe
the impossible. Maybe — what did St Augustine say? — we
become proficient in it by practice, though.'

He peered into the font as if engrossed in the business of
divination. Then he looked up, satisfied with what he had
discerned. 'You know, Vicar, I said I haven't been confirmed.
I've never told anyone this before — except Mike — but I
haven't been christened either. I know you're supposed to
believe before you can be confirmed but they baptize babies,
don't they — and hope they'll one day grow up to believe.
Will you baptize me in this font now?'

'Only one thing stops me doing that.'

He looked momentarily alarmed. I said, 'I don't know
your name.'

'Matthews — Paul Matthews.'

He removed his jacket and tie while I went back into the
vestry to fetch my surplice and stole. There is a wonderfully
named service in the Prayer Book: 'The Ministration of
Baptism to such as are of riper years and able to answer for
themselves.'

The sunlight, fading and brightening, casting rapid

shadows over the walls, made the building seem strangely mobile. As we walked down the path to the lychgate Paul said, 'And if they ask at the hospital what I did today, I shall say I went to a christening.'

LET US NOW PRAISE FAMOUS MEN

I go, once a week, into the village Junior school to lead an assembly for the children. There is a good, big hall with wide windows looking out over the playing fields towards the houses and the church in the background. The children sit down on three sides of a square and I stand on the fourth side by the reading desk with lions carved on it that we rescued from the old schoolhouse. The new school is light, bright, clean and well-equipped with its own gymnasium and a small laboratory but it does not have the atmosphere of the original building. When I first came to Marton, the school was in transit between the old and the new, the yellow bulldozers and the tarmacadaming machines having just laid the last strips of playground and path on the new site. The old building creaked. It also smelt — of dusty books, damp cupboards and ancient furniture. The smell seemed to combine with the sight of children crosslegged, cramped in the long narrow hall and singing hymns from 'Carey Bonner' to Miss Riley at the out-of-tune piano. Is it only nostalgia that makes us prefer such places to their modern substitutes? The children seem happy in their new classrooms furnished with overhead projectors and slimline radiators. In the old school you got told off for sitting on the pipes of the ancient heating system that used to gurgle in the coldest weather. And Miss Riley would have thought an overhead projector was something they used in the Crescent cinema in town.

Perhaps the old school was not, as Mrs Tate the head teacher always pointed out to parents as she showed them round, 'as convenient for the flexible day' as the new open-plan building, but it possessed all the symbolic richness of an old schoolhouse: a sloping roof, a plaque on the outside wall bearing the date 1874, and a bell tower. It also had rotting foundations, rising damp, woodworm and a dilapidated row of outside lavatories.

In the old school the children used to parade into assembly to Miss Riley's ardent plonking of 'Marche Militaire' or, in springtime, 'English Country Gardens'. Now they came in from two directions to marvellous stereophony rendering anything from Schubert's Unfinished to Mahler's Sixth. And there are no pipes in the new hall where the heating is concealed underfloor and the windows are double-glazed. As for the floor itself, it is magnificently smooth and scrupulously polished; no fear of the children getting splinters in their behinds these days, nor of summer dresses becoming embossed with squares of dust. All these things are tangible improvements, so I wonder why it is that many villagers still regret the passing of the old schoolhouse? Is it because the old scenery, even with its primitive plumbing, its rattling windows and the sound of the caretaker shovelling coal into the boiler, was so obviously earthed in tradition and popular mythology about the way a school should be? Perhaps, given time, we shall come to feel just the same about the new place.

Last term I began a series of assemblies on the Lord's Prayer. It was that very snowy winter and, as I stared over the heads of Class I, the children under the white glare of the wide windows looked like mere smudges on an over-exposed photograph. The stereo gave out 'Sleighride' from *Lieutenant Kije*. Children are always rowdy when it snows. In the staffroom Mrs Tate had outlined her meteorological theory of children's behaviour: 'They're best when it's hot. They just want to loll about and go to sleep then. When it's windy they're always losing their scarves and bags — and, of course, in the fog they lose themselves. Rain makes them fidget. But in the snow they simply cannot stop chattering.'

'Now then, what about this?' It is, I have discovered, a help when talking to large groups of children to make sure that your first few words sound arresting without actually saying anything of significance. It gives them a few seconds to realise you have begun. The murmur died away and the hall fell silent, apart from a few sharp and persistent coughs. I continued: 'We say "Our Father who art in heaven". So what d'you think heaven is like?' I rubbed my hands together as if it were cold as I waited for an answer. Jane Kelly in Class II who spoke as if she were reciting a nursery rhyme and swayed as she did so, answered that Heaven is like Christmas because 'you get lots of presents and lots and lots of lovely things to eat.'

The novice assembly-taker must become accustomed to such materialistic predilections, for the hearts of children — no less than those of their elders — frequently seem to be laid up among those treasures which moth and rust corrupt. He must also prepare himself against some fairly surreal side-tracking: 'We went to my Uncle Clifford's on Sunday and his cat has been run over.' That was Jeremy Smail's contribution to the debate about heaven and Christmas. Just then Louise Tanner let out an anguished wail and had to be led away snivelling and sniffing by her class teacher. Heads turned to follow them all the way to the door as if such doings were rare in Marton C. of E. Juniors. Tina Martin, meanwhile, had raised her hand. She hissed urgently through her teeth, trying to catch my attention.

'Mr Mullen, has Jeremy's cat gone to heaven?'

'It wasn't my cat. It was my Uncle Clifford's', said Jeremy, fixing her with a stare. He made it sound as if ownership of the cat in this life was a matter to be taken into consideration with regard to its eternal destiny. 'It was squashed', he went on. 'The wheel went right over it.' His voice was pitched on a dull monotone. Then he brightened as he explained, 'Uncle Clifford had to scrape it off the road with a shovel!'

This information caused great delight among the children. Only the staff, perched strategically on chairs behind each class, looked pale. Mrs Tate clapped her hands, so that for a moment I imagined she was showing appreciation of Jeremy's sad tale. But it was only to reinforce her saying, 'Now, now, Jeremy — I don't think Mr Mullen has come into school to hear stories like that.'

'It's not a story, Miss. It's true!'

In an attempt to lift the discussion a little higher I said, 'I'm sure Jeremy's . . . Jeremy's Uncle Clifford's cat has gone to heaven'. Thus I revealed a certainty about the heavenly life of dumb beasts greater than anything to be found in St Thomas Aquinas or even the Bible. A child's view of heaven is usually filled with so much livestock that it would be churlish to insist on theological rectitude in these affairs. When we read the story of Noah in Class IV no one minded very much that the whole population of the earth, except eight people, perished; but they would have been writing to *Blue Peter* to complain if the Vicar had suggested no animals were saved.

There was a shuffle and a scarcely audible mutter from the front row. Little Sarah Brockbank was furiously mouthing a question. Her expression reminded me of women lip-reading over the noise of looms. 'Speak up Sarah, that's a good girl!' Miss Carnley blushed a little as she spoke, then leaned forward to restrain a big lad in Class II who was trying to kiss his neighbour. Mrs Tate clapped her hands again and Sarah Brockbank was at last given space to say whatever had been worrying her. Her voice was still a whisper. 'We had jelly yesterday. My Mum said we couldn't have jelly because Wayne — that's my brother . . .' (Miss Carnley raised her eyes as if praying for a stay of execution. Wayne had been in her class last year.) '. . . was naughty and went in the flower beds. But then my Auntie Jean came and so we did have jelly.'

'Well, that was nice for you Sarah? And what flavour jelly did you have?' Sarah seemed overcome with the effort of her earlier speech and so she made no reply. A dozen hands went up, however; no doubt their owners wished to let me know their opinions on the subject of jelly. Arrogantly, I brushed them all aside. 'So what do you think — d'you think there's jelly in heaven?' It was my last try to get them back to the Lord's Prayer.

My words were met with absolute silence. Suddenly I knew how those old Music Hall comedians must have felt when they dried on stage. Sarah the squeaky's hand went up again and I glimpsed salvation. 'Well, then Sarah, are you going to tell us all about heaven?'

Her finger went in her mouth and she shook her head slowly. 'Please Mr Mullen, my Auntie Jean has got a budgie and it's green.' No one seemed in the least surprised. It was as if Theatre of the Absurd was the usual mode of communication. There was nothing for it but to join the plot.

'And what's your Auntie Jean's budgie called?'

The child's face took on a stare of the most dazed indifference and she said nothing. Philip McEvany put up his hand and announced in a piping voice that today was his birthday. 'That's nice, Philip. Right then, everyone — we shall sing "Happy Birthday" to Philip. How old are you, Philip?'

'Five,' he said, 'but I'm not four now.'

We were glad of the information. They sang Marton Junior's version of the greeting:

Happy Birthday to you
Squashed tomatoes and stew . . .'

I am sorry to say that images of Jeremy's Uncle Clifford's
cat sneaked back into my mind. Then we said the Lord's
Prayer and a prayer for old people who found it difficult to
get about in the snow. We sang 'Little Drops of Water' and
even as we did so I noticed a constant dripping of the
melted snow which overhung the window. A pale sun half-
appeared racing through thin clouds. Someone rang a bell
and in a minute we were drinking coffee in the staff room.

Mr Stevenson, the ginger-haired teacher of Class III, had
brewed the coffee during his free period. He now sat hugging
the radiator and peering into the *Times Educational Supple-
ment.* The others came in affecting all the symptoms of cold,
as people do whether they are cold or not when there is
snow on the ground. 'There's a job here,' said Stevenson,
'"Teacher of Infants. Embassy and other diplomatic staff
children. The English School, Athens." Pay's better than we
get as well.'

Louise Carnley, unravelling the wrapper of a chocolate
biscuit, began a long reminiscence about the time she went
to Greece with Gerald. Ingrid Tate was staring into a large
diary. Without raising her eyes she said, 'That was in the
days before your Gerald became high and mighty.' She
made an exaggerated regal gesture, then for my benefit she
added, 'Louise's "ex" — he is still "ex" I take it, Louise? —
he's the new General Infants Adviser for the Local Education
Authority. We're expecting him today. Perhaps you'd like to
meet him, Mr Mullen?'

'That's if he can make it through the snow on those
country roads', said Louise giving the chocolate biscuit a
severe look but continuing to eat it nonetheless.

'Janet Dickenson's mother says will we let her out at half-past two — she's got to go to the dentist's', said Colin Stevenson as if to prove that non-sequential dialogue was not the monopoly of the children.

'Who's on playground duty?' The headmistress had put down the diary and she stood hands on hips by the window.

'Elsie,' said Louise and Colin at once.

Just then Miss Riley in her thick framed glasses and woolly hat trudged into view followed by a crowd of loudly lamenting children. One of them was covered in snow and weeping while the others seemed to be competing with one another in the business of making excuses. Elsie Riley stopped in her tracks and, like a slimmed down mirror image of Mrs Tate, stood still with her hands on her hips, her face twisted in mock horror. All this we observed as a pantomime, for little sound penetrated the double glazed windows and the drama took place half-way across the playground.

Abruptly, they left off their complaints and recriminations at the exciting new vision of a car stuck in the entrance to the drive. 'If I've told them once, I've told them a thousand times, not to make slides in the driveway,' said Mrs Tate. In a lower voice she added, 'Good God — it's Gerald Fairbrother!'

People left their chairs and began to rinse coffee cups. Stevenson picked up a pile of exercise books and gave them a professional glance. He left the room, muttering industriously, also inaudibly as he had stuck a marker pen between his teeth. Louise threw the wrapper in the bin and made a face into her hand mirror as she dabbed her lips with a handkerchief. She said quietly to Mrs Tate: 'You can send him in to me any time. Not that I think he'll want to come, particularly.'

Outside, a gang of kids were leaning hard on the new

General Adviser's car as the wheels whizzed and whined over the snow to no effect. As he had slowed down to enter, the front wheels had slipped on the icy patch, causing the rear end to swing round and lodge in the drifts by the gate. Gerald Fairbrother sat at the wheel looking so intense that I imagined he might be trying to edge the car forward by sheer will-power.

It was at this moment that George Mulberry, the school caretaker, began a lackadaisical stroll across the playground towards the scene of distress. Fairbrother noticed him and, seeming to sense hope at last, gave him a thin smile through the windscreen. George grimaced. He stopped and stared at the car as if it had no business — which in a sense it hadn't — to be where it was. Then he frightened the children away and made a sign to Miss Riley who positioned herself by the rear wheel. He made a face at Fairbrother and waved his hand from side to side like a disappointed teacher chastising a frequent offender. Fairbrother looked less sanguine. The caretaker took out a newspaper from under his brown smock. He held it before the driver's eyes for a moment as if conducting some sort of test. Then he opened the pages and laid the separate sheets under the orbit of the front wheel. He pointed at Elsie Riley and nodded at Gerald Fairbrother. The car sped forward with ease and curled away silently over the thick snow to the parking area. Children lining the square applauded and threw their hats in the air. Miss Riley's cheeks turned pinker than ever, George bent to retrieve his newspaper, folded it with great care and sauntered off towards his own house.

Gerald Fairbrother came into the staff room oozing gratitude and bonhomie. 'Good fellow you've got there, Mrs Tate. Don't know where I'd have been without him.'

Whereupon George Mulberry entered unexpectedly. 'Still stuck in the blinking snow, that's where you'd be, mister.

Some folks have no more sense than they're born with —
revving and screeching away like that never gets nobody
nowhere. Only thing to do is to turn off the engine, leave
the beggar in gear and shove some paper under the wheel
like I did. Then she'll slip out, smooth as you like.' He made
a movement with both hands like someone beginning the
breast stroke.

'I'm sure Mr Fairbrother is very grateful for all you did,
George', said Mrs Tate.

'I certainly am,' said the Adviser, blowing on his fingers
and rubbing his hands together.

'Then you want to look a bit more lively in future.' He
turned from his censure of the senior official to fix the
headmistress with a sharp stare. 'And you want to look out
as well. When I came in here at seven o'clock this morning,
all of them windows was wide open. Snow was blowing
about all over the place in here.' After giving us all another
disgusted look he left.

He was a living illustration of the mythology of caretakers
— that it is they, and not the teachers, still less the Advisory
Staff with smart briefcases and modern theories, who have
real power and authority in schools. I thought of myself in
front of that assembly, trying to teach the Lord's Prayer; I
remembered the squeamish looks on the faces of the staff
when Jeremy Smail described the demise of his Uncle
Clifford's cat; I remembered Mrs Tate's own words about
the uncontrollability of children in snowy weather; and, if I
shut my eyes, I could still see Elsie Riley trying to exercise
discipline over the playground quarrellers. Against this
pageant of failures, middling successes and muddling
through, I set the power and authority of George Mulberry
as in my mind's eye I saw him strolling like a giant in this
childish world, closing windows after careless schoolteachers,
delivering high and mighty representatives of the Education

Office from the results of their errors, presenting *his* school clean, orderly, 'a picture' as Mrs Tate said.

As Mrs Tate also said, 'Behind every successful head teacher there is an efficient caretaker.'

One who made sure that the General Infants Adviser did not stick in the mud and slush on his way out.

12

WITH THIS RING

Tuesday evenings I try to keep for wedding interviews — a pleasant enough job, which involves sitting in the study reading or listening to a concert while waiting for the couples to arrive. One hot summer evening when I was torn between the ending of *Middlemarch* and the desire to go into the kitchen for that can of cold lager, I heard the click of the gate and the sound of feet on the gravel path. He was very tall and wearing a light summer suit. She reached not quite as high as his shoulder and she seemed to be running along beside him. I knew her, of course: Sally Greenslade, the postman's daughter from the isolated cottage half-way between Marton and Bradburn. Her father had sung in the choir since music was invented and even deputised for the organist in August but, as he said, 'I'll leave it to Duffield to play for our Sally's wedding. I reckon she's going to ask for something funny.'

Something funny it was to be, as I soon found out. Sally and her fiancé — who was not from these parts as you might guess from his name, Owen Thomas Williams — were squeezed up against each other on the sofa, her hands disappearing into his. She said, 'D'you think we could have 'A Funny Kind of Love', Vicar?' I confess to having suppressed the first remark that came into mind. Owen Thomas leaned forward so that his hands almost touched the carpet. 'It's a classical piece really,' he said with lilting enthusiasm, 'I reckon it's by Clementi.' He pronounced the last syllable to rhyme with 'Dai'. 'And if that's not possible, we'd like 'A Lighter Shade of Pale'. Sally fingered the strap on her bag and sneaked a glance at her Owen Thomas. I had visions of George Duffield busting out of the vestry, sheets of pop music in his hand, expostulating all over the chancel about the sacking of Wagner and Mendelssohn.

'Oh, but we want the proper — you know, the usual, to come out to —' 'Da, Da, da-dee-dum-dum-dum', interrupted the Welshman in true national style, 'That's the Wedding March, innit?'

Having settled that the choice of music was, within reason and the conspicuous virtuosity of George Duffield, a matter for the bride and groom, we passed to more essential matrimonial issues such as flowers and photographs. They wanted what every wedding couple wants: a picture of themselves kneeling at the altar. In the olden days, vicars never allowed this, but in these times of our sophistication when colour movies and videoed nuptials are all the rage, I have not heard of anyone forbidding a snapshot. I did mention, as a gobbet of historical interest, that it was not many years since the Archbishops had issued a circular to all the clergy, informing us that photographs during church services were officially disapproved.

'All right for him 'innit?' sang Owen Thomas, 'We can't have our snap from a Brownie 127 but every time the Archbishop goes to church you can't move for television cameras.' He pronounced the word 'Archbishop' with a Welsh Baptist's disdain for showy prelates who were no better than papal fifth-columnists in the Church of England. We agreed on the standard altar-pic and one of them coming down the aisle to the Duffield-Mendelssohn.

'What I really want to know', said Williams, as if our twenty minutes discussion of exits and entrances had been mere preamble, 'is how many hymns we can have.'

'My Mum wants 'O Perfect Love' but I'd rather have 'Love Divine' said Sally with confidence, seeming to grow larger as she spoke.

'Well,' I said, 'have as many as you like but watch out for "Praise My Soul" if your bridesmaids are on the plump side.'

I told them of that wedding long ago in the days of my first curacy, when I got the giggles because there we all were belting out 'Father-like He tends and spares us; well our feeble frame He knows', and, singing louder than most, were three of the buxomest bridesmaids ever to loom before the chancel step.

I did not tell them the more *risqué* anecdote which was part of our old college principal's crash course for Ordinands: Part 69 — How to Conduct a Wedding Interview. I can still see the old boy, peering over the top of his glasses, his lips twisted into that familiar expression that could have been either a smile or a wince: 'Don't forget to advise them not to go too far on the first night. Edith and I went as far as Edinburgh — and it was far too far!' And his face remained in that fixed grin while the assembled ordinands tried to transmute lewd delight into restrained laughter. Whether the old boy knew not or knew very well what he said was a matter for endless speculation over the coffee cups after Compline; but he told the same story every year and the chaplain often used to tease the final year men by asking them if the principal had yet told them how far they could go.

Weddings themselves usually turn out to be a lot less fuss than all the preparations. The groom and his man sit like a condemned prisoner and his guard on the front pew — except that the condemned prisoner is allowed a smoke. There are so many white hats the nave looks like a regatta, and everywhere is the aroma of dutch courage. The bride's more distant relations squint out of their eye corners at the groom's people on the other side of the aisle. Duffield pierces their conviviality with an icy stare when he thinks their gossip is drowning his voluntary. Eventually there are 'oo's!' and 'ah's', and sentimental smiles of old ladies in choir and congregation as the appearance of the bride brings on a fit of reminiscence or, in some cases, of imagination.

The brides themselves usually arrive two minutes late and quaking with cold rather than apprehension. Our church porch is draughty and I have welcomed more than one bride in a snowstorm. Bride and groom settle down once they begin making their vows but I always feel sorry for the bride's father. He is not losing a daughter but gaining an overdraft, apart from which he is the only person to whom a question not requiring an answer is addressed during the proceedings. If there are to be photographs in church, then let one be of this poor man as he is startled by the challenge: 'Who giveth this woman to be married to this man?' In music hall jokes, in American films and even perhaps in ordinary expectation, the answer is 'I do'. In fact the bride's father is not required to say anything but simply to offer the arm of his daughter to the vicar. The pressure of this short silence, however, is such that it cannot be resisted by mere choreography and, as he proffers his girl, the giver-away will usually mutter some sort of response which may indeed be 'I do', but it could just as well be 'It's me', 'Righto' or 'Here you are then'.

Of course, the dramatic cliché would be for the best man to forget the ring. I have never known this to happen. Best men always walk about on wedding days with one hand in the jacket pocket, so that you might conclude this posture to be a congenital affectation among them, or else a qualification for their office. Once having delivered the ring from its little box, the best man recovers again his normal ambidexterity. But I have known the clasp on the box to stick, and to remain stuck though pecked at by nervous fingers for two or three minutes. When some such minor irritation as this happens in a wedding service, it is always regarded as a catastrophe. Bride and groom stare terrified ahead as if a curse has fallen upon their nuptials, a delusion which, once communicated to the rest of the congregation by the fumbling and delay, gains in strength until it becomes a generalized panic. At such a crisis I once heard, from no more than three rows back, the lugubrious mutter: 'It looks as if she isn't going to go through with it.' In practice (as opposed to nightmare) the catch always comes undone and there is a sigh of relief such as follows a long putt on the eighteenth green not a mile from our church.

And I have never known any objection at those stark words 'If any man can shew any just cause, etc. let him now speak or else hereafter for ever hold his peace.' I did once, however, have a four-year-old page boy ask me, after the ceremony, why had I been offering the people peppermints and why he did not get one. It was half-way through the best man's speech before I located the assonance: '. . . any just cause or *impediment*.'

At the wedding of Sally the postman's girl to the massive Welshman there occurred an event which I had secretly dreaded for years. The day itself broke clear and bright, the churchyard mellow in its autumn colours and fresh after recent light rain. There was nothing to suggest catastrophe. Owen Thomas was in his place by ten minutes before noon and looking, I am bound to say, like the introit they had finally settled on: 'A Lighter Shade of Pale'. The best man had that faraway look of one who would rather be at Cardiff Arms Park than at this local match, but I noticed with satisfaction that his left hand had assumed the appropriate posture. When I asked if he had remembered the ring, he replied without first making a formal search.

A flurry of white movement at the lychgate signalled the

arrival of Sally and her father. Duffield was in position, scowling at the murmuring congregation and steeling himself to vamp his way through that 'Lighter Shade'. Ebullient toddlers were snatched back into the pews from where they had been scuttering about in the aisle. Sally's sister Emma was pacing about the porch trying to silence her screaming infant, the lately-christened Gary Michael: 'Doo, doo, dum! Auntie Sally doesn't want to hear all that din on her wedding day, does she now?' No doubt she did not, but, if she would marry, then hear it she must. All the usual questions: 'When do I lift my veil?' 'Am I on the right side?' 'Shall I give my bouquet to the bridesmaids as soon as we get to the chancel step?' Old Tom Greenslade looked weatherbeaten, nervous, proud. He gave me a huge wink then wiped all over his face with a new white handkerchief.

In no time at all we had — as it said in the unsung words of that pop-introit —'skipped the light fandango'; I had required and charged them both, etc.; Tom had muttered his needless 'I do'; the lovely couple had willingly uttered 'I will'; troths had been eloquently plighted. I held out the Prayer Book so that the best man could place the ring on it. The catch on the little case opened without hitch and his fingers tightly gripped the little circle of gold. Alas, not tightly enough, for the ring slipped from his grasp and with two or three melodious clinks bounced its way down the honeycomb of the central heating grille.

I thought Sally was about to cry. It was obvious that she thought the marriage must now be off. The bridesmaids clapped their hands to their mouths. Tom, who had been day-dreaming, awoke to mumble 'What's up?' Owen Thomas stared down the black grille as if into a Welsh Baptist's hell. I noticed that Sally, as I had advised her, was wearing her engagement ring on her right hand. I tried my most nonchalant smile. 'Now, there's nothing to worry about

. . .' I felt like the pilot on the old films who steps out of his cockpit to reassure his passengers, knowing all the time that the starboard engine has packed up. '. . . Sally, you give him your engagement ring.' She did so — though not without first staring in horror at the grille as if it were a magnet which could easily attract this second ring also. And so we went through the ceremony using this handy substitute.

In the vestry for the signing of the registers, both bride and groom wanted to know whether the wedding was valid without the ring.

'But you did have a ring!'

'Yes, but not a wedding ring.'

'And what *is* a wedding ring? The Prayer Book says "and the man shall give unto the woman a ring" — and that's what you did.'

Still they seemed to imagine that, as a consequence, the marriage might lack something in the way of durability. Mrs Greenslade gave the poor best man a few narrow looks and seemed to be within a whisker of asking if he had been in 'The Acorn' before the service. He looked as if he could do with being in 'The Acorn' now.

In fact, it was only a ten minute job to remove the grille and poke about in the shallow trench for the ring. Arnold Clay the verger had his sleeves rolled up at once and he even delivered the ring to the reception on his way home. Three weeks later, I asked Sally and Owen Thomas to stay behind after Holy Communion and I blessed their gold ring. But we did it in the Lady Chapel, well away from the grille. Nowadays, a carefully fitted piece of black hardboard sticks to the underside of that hazard — and this has been sufficient to guarantee that no ring has fallen since.

13

SEEING WE ARE COMPASSED ABOUT . . .

Edward Benson's family had lived in Marton since the time of the Civil War and they had sat every Sunday in the same pew since St Luke's was restored in between the wars of our own century. The last of the Bensons had never married and, since Bessie's death in 1977, Edward was the only surviving member of the family. Bessie's name was a legend in the village and beyond — for years leader of the Parish Council, buxom Bessie with the bright red face and a voice of deep contralto resonance. She used to bring her riding whip into the Council meetings and all the village knew her as 'someone big with horses' — a resolute woman, uncrushably optimistic even in the face of the most forbidding tasks. She would sit in the oak armchair in the village hall and meet any objection with such a particular intonation of 'Pardon?' that the objector wished he had never opened his mouth. But she was not without humour. Children — out of earshot — would imitate her laugh. There were more jokes about Bessie Benson than there were about the parson and the publican put together. For twenty-five years she *was* Marton. When she died the whole village turned out and there was standing room only in church for the first time since the Armistice service in 1919.

Edward, by contrast — you might almost say by necessary contrast since he and his sister had lived under the one roof all those years — was a quiet man, softly spoken and with a gift for reticence. He pottered about with that air of fragile elegance which made you think he was not long for this world; but he outlived his strenuous sister for whom he was cook, cleaner, clerk and confidant. If you mentioned his sister he would give you a thin smile and say 'Ah, Bessie!' in the tone of one about to begin a long anecdote; but he would add nothing to those two words spoken with a mixture of awe and indulgence. Despite appearances, no one made jokes about the couple as if they were the originals for the domineering woman and the weedy little man on seaside postcards. Everyone knew how much Bessie had relied on her brother and, if she spoke his name in public, her voice became quiet and respectful. He nursed her in her last illness with a tenderness that was apparent as soon as you stepped into the old farmhouse. In his soft, expressive voice he read to her from the Psalms through many winter nights. He was with her when she died. His bony fingers turned whiter as he gripped the bedrail. But his mourning was mixed with an overwhelming sense of thankfulness for their years of affectionate comradeship.

The pattern of his life barely altered after Bessie's death: early rising to light the fires and exercise the dog, a mid-morning visit to the stables and on Sundays the Holy Communion. The rituals of country life blended easily with those of the Church. I have found that there are two main sorts of churchgoers: those who take their religion for granted, not in a slovenly or ungrateful style but as one takes for granted belonging to a family; and those who not only practise their faith but who reflect on their practice. Bessie had been of the first sort, a cheerful Christian woman, her name at the top of each annual flower list, a regular at the Parochial Church Council meetings and willing to help out with the endless fund-raising events. Edward was of the second type, diligent in prayer, scrupulous to attend the mid-week Communion and to be there on all the special feasts and fasts. He preserved the old-fashioned Christian countryman's habit of referring to the time or the season by its place in the Church Calendar. 'It must be last Michaelmas since I saw old so-and-so . . . He came on All Souls and stayed until Christmas.' And so on. Yet he was never pretentiously pious in that cloying, sanctimonious style associated with George Eliot's Methodists and Dickens' undertakers. He spoke of religious observances as a natural part of life and he was able to do this in an entirely unforced way because for Edward nature itself was charged with religious significance. He was the only person in Marton who came to Confession. He came three times a year at his own asking. Afterwards, as we walked away from church he would remark on some new phenomenon in such a way that you imagined he was personally responsible for it: pointing with his ebony-handled stick towards the orchards on the south side and promising there would be a good harvest of plums; remembering to the day when the swallows returned; spotting some minor imperfection in a piece of church property — 'That bottom hinge on the old gate is coming loose. We'll see what we can do.' The altar in St Luke's was a lovely piece of Jacobean oak; it received its ritual oiling every year from Edward on — as most befitting ceremonies of oil — Maundy Thursday.

Last Easter the table was not done, and Edward was not in church at the festival Eucharist but lay instead in a side ward in York General Hospital. He was in church on Tuesday in Holy Week for our usual Lent study group; one of my last recollections was of him sitting on the front pew in the Lady chapel, muffled against the draught in his charcoal overcoat and check scarf and doodling on the bare boards with the point of his stick as we remembered our Lord's Passion in the Garden. I remember thinking at the time that if Edward had been one of the disciples he would have summoned the strength to 'watch one hour'. But in his case, too, the spirit was indeed willing and the flesh weak.

On Wednesday morning he suffered a heart attack while
shaving and he was discovered 'all purple and breathless' by
Mrs Grant when she came in to collect the laundry. She
telephoned the vicarage at nine o'clock: 'They've just taken
him, Vicar, Mr Benson. He did look strange — a wicked
colour. His heart I've no doubt. I do hope they can do
something for him. It reminded me of Herbert — he went
like that at the finish. But you never know — they can do all
sorts these days.'

The shape of the thoughts which strike us at such
moments is unaccountable. All I can remember is something
approaching disbelief at the pallid features of Papa Benson
ever turning 'a wicked colour'. When I saw him he was quiet
and still. An oxygen cylinder stood by his bed like a sentry.
A West Indian nurse came in and took his pulse twice while
I was there and the bald, overworked, heart specialist
explained in his nasal accent that it had been a very close
call. I sat in the wicker chair under the window and watched
the comings and goings in the railway yard below. It was the
sort of cold, bright spring day that belonged on a watercolour, the clouds thin, grey like a tapestry and ready to
pour, the sunlight coming in fits and starts as if it was being
squeezed through a bottleneck. Edward did not move. His
mouth was open slightly, his bottom lip moist but his
breathing silent. For the first time his familiar joke rang true:
'I'm turned seventy now you know, Father — that's borrowed time!'

I called in to the ward again after the service on Maundy
Thursday and again in the evening of Good Friday. Those
services had not seemed the same. The Bensons' empty pew
was like a presumption, as if a man's will should be read
before the event. On the Friday he was able to talk a little.
There was this worry — I had been expecting it — about his
confession and Easter Communion. 'You've been searched

out quite enough this week, Edward. Let's simply use the standard Confession from the Prayer Book'. Just before noon on Easter Day I brought the sacrament to his bedside and the young black nurse received it with him. By this time there were so many greetings cards around his bed that it seemed more like Christmas than Easter. By the following Wednesday he was sitting up in bed and pronouncing stoic grace over the hospital food. Beyond mere contempt for the injunction not to talk too much, Edward suddenly became more voluble; supported by his mountain of pillows and with palms turned downward over the immaculate counterpane he would hold forth as if time were spring and words were flowers. But the mode of his conversation was changed; added to his usual chatty style and the happy facility of contriving unusual interest out of routine events, there was a fresh intimacy, a new willingness, almost a necessity, to talk about himself and his past. The famous reticence seemed to give way to a warmth and directness that was both unselfregarding and unashamed.

'You know, Father, what I always wanted was a son — or a daughter — children at any rate, more than one. I might have had them, too. I courted a young lady from Whitby before the war. But I hesitated. And, you know, distance was an item in those days and, what with my responsibilities at home — one thing and another — I couldn't get to see her as often as I liked. She married someone else, of course, and they went to live in New Zealand.' His face took on a distant expression and he gazed over my shoulder, out of the window as if New Zealand lay in that direction. He clenched his hands and the thin smile returned. 'Well, I had my chance, didn't I? It never came again. We'd plenty to do on the farm in those days. Mother and father were alive and Bessie went and joined the WRAF. Strange that she never married either. We never talked about it, you know. Funny how these things come back to you — at my time of life as well! Borrowed time you know, Father. Borrowed time!'

One of the other nurses stood at the bottom of his bed like a proprietor waiting to shut up shop. 'Time you had a rest, Mr Benson. You'll be tiring out the Vicar!'

'It's only words, my dear,' he replied. 'A song at twilight, eh?'

At the beginning of May he was home again with instructions to act his age, to take a reasonable amount of gentle exercise, but to rest whenever he felt even slightly tired. Gradually he regained his strength and that summer he even seemed to attract a little colour to his cheeks — of the non-wicked variety. He seemed himself to personify the summer, sitting in his doorway with his white hat and his stick, and looked after permanently now by Mrs Grant, who had moved from her house in the village into one of the old farm cottages. Mrs Grant's husband was a short-contract worker for a company that laid pipelines in various parts of the country, and so he was away from home for long periods. His son, Toby, had got to know Edward during the school holidays and, whenever you passed, you would see the two of them deep in conversation over some small treasure Toby had fetched from the woods or the bank of the stream. The boy called him 'Mr Edward', as every shop-keeper in the village discovered upon being asked by the breathless Toby for 'Mr Edward's newspaper' . . . 'Mr Edward's groceries', his writing paper, his stamps, his paper-clips and everything that was Mr Edward's. The relationship flourished to their mutual benefit. Toby was learning the piano and he would play his pieces on Bessie Benson's gothic upright while the old man nodded in the corner.

At first I took the sacrament to Edward's home every Sunday after the morning service, but as he came to feel stronger, he hankered after his own pew again. There was no question of his returning to his lifelong habit of tramping across the fields first thing on a Sunday morning, so one of the sidesmen would collect him in the car. He was as devout as ever and it went ill with him when he was told he should sit rather than kneel. You got the impression that he had to summon all his charity to forgive his nurses. In other respects there was a bigger change in his behaviour. The austere Anglo-Catholicism gave way to a warmer, more relaxed attitude in Church. The concentrated attention and ritualistic observances continued as before, but it was ritual with a human face. He would greet people on his way in, whereas his disciplined habit had always been to keep strict silence until after Communion. He took more interest in the young children who went off during the sermon to work with their Sunday school teachers in the church hall, and the time of their return to race up the aisle for a blessing at the Administration was a highlight for the old man. I knew that in the past, along with a few other older members of the congregation, he had merely tolerated the presence of the children and regarded them as a hindrance to the business of devotion. Now he beamed encouragement at them as they came back from the altar rail, and over coffee in the hall he would produce toffees and sneak them into the children's hands while their parents were lost in conversation.

Just after the Harvest, Edward took a turn for the worse. Mrs Grant telephoned one evening and I could tell by her quiet, resigned voice that she believed the end would not be long delayed. I can remember the evening clearly. The ecclesiastical harvest rarely coincides exactly with the real harvest and the men were still burning stubble in the corners of the fields. It was a dry autumn and the flames burned high in the dusk. A veil of smoke drifted level with the treetops, and just above it the harvest moon hung in the darkening sky like a sovereign produced from a handkerchief.

'Are the men burning stubble then? I thought I could smell it.' These were his first words when I arrived. He was sitting up in bed as I had seen him in hospital and he looked rather better than I had imagined from Mrs Grant's tone. When I told him that they were almost finished burning off the ends of the fields, he nodded, satisfied — like a pilot just given a piece of information vital for the voyage. Edward guided his life by the Church's calendar, but he knew the countryman's diary as well. Even in the age of television and harvesters programmed by microchips, these people still go less by the abstract accountancy of numbered dates and more by the timing of the events on the land — 'burning off', 'putting in the winter barley', and so on.

Mrs Grant was fussing round the bed, lightly brushing away imaginary dust, filling Edward's water glass and talking in that exaggerated voice which people reserve for addressing domestic pets and invalids.

'Now the Vicar's come, Mr Benson. I told you he would. I'll leave you be for a while. I'll only be next door if you want me.' She gave the bedside table another unnecessary flick of the duster and then departed into the kitchen.

'Toby sat with me for a bit, but it's his bedtime now, bless him. I just wanted a word, Father, about money for the Church.' The old man winced and hunched up his shoulders suddenly as if he had been struck by an unreachable itch in the middle of his back. I helped him move into a more comfortable position. All the while he held out a restraining finger as if forbidding me to raise any objection to his speech until he had quite finished. He coughed. 'Look, it's not a fortune, but I'd like it to be enough for a new set of altar frontals and vestments to match . . .' His voice fell away and he suddenly frowned as you would if you lost your place in a complicated counting game. 'Toby', he began again '— and his mother — he's been a good friend to me, has Toby. He reads to me you know. And he plays the piano. He'll be due for Confirmation next year. I would like to be there, but I don't suppose I shall . . . except as part of the invisible choir.'

We said the Lord's Prayer, the Magnificat and the collect that begins 'Lighten our darkness. . . .' It was dark when I left him sleeping. Mrs Grant was all silence and gesticulations. She walked across the yard to my car and whispered that she would telephone at once 'if there's any change'.

She rang at ten o'clock the next morning. When I arrived, Dr Broughton was just leaving. He said the old man had died peacefully. Toby was sitting downstairs in the rocking chair with a glass of orange juice beside him. He was making a show of reading his book. When I entered he began to cry. I put my prayer book on the table and sat down. 'You know, Toby, Mr Edward wouldn't like you to cry. He's gone to be with . . .'

He answered loudly through his tears. 'I know where he's gone. He told me where he was going. I know all about it. Mr Edward used to tell me all about it when I'd been reading to him. Paradise, that's where he's gone. Just like that thief on the cross — that's what he said — the one that said he was sorry.'

Later, Mrs Grant told me that Toby had been reading to the old man the morning when he died. The following year the Confirmation took place on 12th May — Rogation, as Edward would have said. We used the new altar frontal, and Toby was presented with a Bible from his parents and a prayer book signed by Edward Benson. On the old man's instructions, Mrs Grant had kept it out of sight until the big day. It was inscribed with the text, 'Seeing we are compassed about with so great a cloud of witnesses.'

14

THE DEVIL AND ALL HIS WORKS

In the winter months we have a discussion group which meets in the vicarage on Tuesday evenings. It is as if for an hour and a half, the capacity to order the fate of God's universe has devolved upon Marton. Indeed, even to refer to the universe as belonging to God is to beg an issue which is certainly not begged on Tuesdays in the vicarage where no opinion, however heretical, is refused a hearing.

In fact, it was Miss Cramp at one of our last meetings who raised the question of who controls the world. Miss Cramp is an alert and wiry woman, a spinster aged about sixty — the sort who remains vigilant even when asleep. She said, 'It looks to me that the Devil himself is in charge of the world, not God.' And she stared about her as if daring the Devil to leap from behind one of the comfortable chairs and challenge her opinion.

Jack Kelsey the farmer took it upon himself to answer the irascible spinster. As he did so, he slowly raised his hands in front of him and held them there where they would have come in very useful to a woman winding wool. 'It all depends the way you work at it . . .' In truth Jack's own eyesight was not all that it might have been and, as he lowered his hands, he knocked a teacup off the little table. He was all red-faced apology. Amid the fluster of assistance, Miss Cramp sat back in her chair, a look of serene triumph on her face as if the mishap were proof of the Devil's mastery — even over vicarage parlours. Linda Sharrat, the latest of our teenagers to become engaged, gathered up the fragments and whipped them away into the kitchen.

I said, 'You were saying, Jack?'

'You must let me know when Mrs Mullen has found a replacement for that cup. I should pay her for it. Clumsy fool that I am. I was just . . .' And he performed a slow replay of his misdemeanour. We looked more like a charades party than a discussion group.

'He was saying', said Linda returning from the kitchen, 'that the Devil is not in charge.'

'Not exactly that, Linda', replied Jack in his ponderous way and making sure he kept his hands safely on his knees. 'I meant I don't know as anyone's in charge. It all depends how you look at it. If it's a fine day when I go out across Low Field, I say to myself "God's in his heaven and all's right with Marton." But if I go out and weather's all mucky and the field like a quagmire — or else it's all frozen over . . .' He made a slow horizontal movement with his hand but, remembering the earlier havoc, he interrupted the gesture and replaced the wayward limb on his knee. '. . . then I think "The Devil makes the weather on my farm".' He seemed disappointed with the impact of his speech and he looked ruefully at his hand as if powers of persuasion were muscular powers — which, of course, in Jack Kelsey's case, they were.

Mr Beamish the bank manager sat on the sofa with his wife, the demure Letitia who was never called 'Letty' but very properly 'Mrs Beamish'; and 'Letitia' by her even more proper husband. She said, 'I think all these films about devils and demons and exorcisms have a very bad influence.' She looked straight ahead as she spoke, her hands clenched rather than folded in her lap, her legs touching at the knees and ankles as if they were welded together.

'Oh, I don't know', said the relaxed Gordon Beamish. 'Entertainment's only entertainment, it's not theology.' He turned to his wife whose forward stare never wavered. 'We went to see some pretty wild stuff when we were a bit younger, eh, Letitia?'

The association of prim Letty with anything wild was a strain on the imagination.

'But do you think there is a Devil really, Mr Mullen?' Linda had resumed her usual posture, lounging on the carpet with one leg tucked under her, picking at the buckle on her sandal as she spoke.

'Of course there's a Devil! One minute's experience of the world and it's obvious.' Miss Cramp answered fiercely as if Linda were herself at least partly responsible for the Devil's existence. It would have been no surprise had she continued, 'You young people sprawling on the floor like that — no wonder there's a Devil!'

But it was Jack Kelsey, having recovered his theological nerve, who spoke next: 'Worst weather of all — though folks who don't know farming would never guess — is when it freezes over for weeks at a time and you have the deuce of a job feeding the animals. Just providing regular watering is an all day job.'

There was silence while this piece of climatic demonology was assimilated by the rest of the company.

'Do you believe that people can be possessed, Vicar?' It seemed a surprising question to come from Letitia. 'Because I knew someone who was possessed. They'd been playing with that game where you put the letters of the alphabet in a circle and turn a glass upside-down . . .'

'We played that at Steve Latham's party', said Linda, 'and we didn't half scare ourselves. Julie Coather went all cold and everybody felt funny. Then Steve's mum came in and asked what we'd been up to. When she saw the glass and the letters she nearly went mad.'

Letitia turned her head sharply like a watchful bird. 'That's what happened to this person I knew. She went mad. She had to go in The Retreat and nobody could do anything with her. Then they got a priest to come and exorcise her and she started to get well after that.'

Jack Kelsey leaned back in his chair and took a huge white handkerchief to his nose. 'I don't know about all this exercizing. You know what they say "The Devil provides work for idle hands . . ."'

'I don't think Letitia quite meant that, Mr Kelsey. Did you, dear?' But she had returned to her fixed forward stare and she seemed hardly to hear her husband's remark.

I said, 'Does the time we live in have anything to do with what we think about devils? I mean, in Jesus' day everyone took devils for granted and exorcists were ten a penny. I guess that our modern methods of psychotherapy would have sounded as fanciful to Jesus' contemporaries as exorcism sounds to us.'

'But it was what worked on . . . this person I knew', said Mrs Beamish.

Miss Cramp looked cross. She was not cross, though. I knew that look. It was just her way of being emphatic. 'Look, the Devil isn't someone you can clear up by exorcism. If that could be done, we would soon be rid of all evil in the world. But you know as well as I do, the world gets more wicked every day.' This time she spared Linda the fierce glance.

'Well, I don't know about that Miss Cramp', said Gordon, ascribing to himself something worse than the title of heretic by dissenting from the alert spinster's doctrine, 'but I'll grant that evil is not so easily got rid of. The Devil tempts even the best people. I mean, he even tempted Jesus in the wilderness didn't he? — "Make these stones bread." '

'What d'you think then?' said Linda. 'D'you think the Devil just appeared to Christ in the wilderness — just like that? I saw a film once where the Devil isn't a creature with horns and a tail but an English gentleman.'

Miss Cramp's keen face broke into a luxurious smile which indicated that she had been acquainted with devils of this sort.

'And yet, you see, we pray "Lead us *not* into temptation",' I said. 'But Jesus was tempted — even led into temptation by the Spirit of God if Matthew 4 is anything to go by. I've always been puzzled by that bit. As you say, Gordon, Jesus was tempted but he teaches us to pray "Lead us not into temptation".'

'Well now, I'll ask you a question,' said Jack stirring himself and taking a long time to fit the handkerchief back in his pocket. 'Would any of you spend a night in yon church by yourself?' He substituted his pipe for his handkerchief and he seemed to point the stem accusingly in Miss Cramp's direction. He then began a long lugubrious tale about how he was once coming home through the graveyard late at night and was convinced he saw a dark figure standing by one of the carved angels. ''Course,' he said, 'I was only a young man in those days.' The words contained a fine ambiguity, for the information added about his age at the time of this extraordinary vision seemed designed both to add credibility to the tale and offer an excuse for it.

I went over to draw the curtains. There through the window was the image of our symposium reflected out among the dark bushes. Thirty yards away was the churchyard of Jack Kelsey's reminiscence, the monuments at odd angles so that they resembled avant-garde sculptures in a darkened museum. I remained there gazing towards the lamp at the corner of the drive and trying to discern whether it was still raining. Jack's voice seemed to lull the whole group and there was the atmosphere of Christmas and ghost stories — the sort of atmosphere in which you relaxed and allowed the words of the story to become associated with whatever common object in the room your eyes fixed upon. Miss Cramp looked into the fire. Linda was fascinated by her own fingernails. The bank manager looked at his watch, then looked at his wife who continued to look straight ahead. Jack's gestures were as generous as his imagination and when he said '. . . went right up to the stone where the figure had been standing . . .' his arms traced an expansive curve as if he were Moses preaching eloquently to the Children of Israel.

When he had finished there was a long silence which seemed to say, 'Now then, and what did you think of that?' Miss Cramp stood up and said she had to be going. Her kitty had been alone all day and all evening, so she must go and give it some milk. Once she had left the others seized upon aspects of Jack's story and related them to adventures of their own. The rest of the evening was passed as among fishermen outbidding one another on the issue of whose missed catch was the largest. Linda had 'definitely felt things' on a number of occasions and she said she thought the supernatural was just as natural as anything else after all. Letitia was sure there must be something. Even her husband confessed to having felt 'a bit odd' some evenings when he had been forced to work late and alone at the bank. At half-past nine they fumbled among the pegs in the hall for coats, hats and scarves while Jack Kelsey told us all that he had 'heard some tales about the old vicarage as well'. The weather itself had turned melodramatic and there was some rather forced hilarity among the guests as they stood on the doorstep. Linda ran off to her home which was just around the corner. The others took to their cars and edged out into the village street. There was a moment when Beamish's headlights caught Jack Kelsey turning the key in his car door and he looked like an apparition from his own story, his red face unusually white in the glare, his large overcoated figure bent black as he fiddled with the lock.

Next morning Barbara and I went to the supermarket. She said, 'You were unusually quiet last night. There wasn't a sound as I passed the study. Then old Jack Kelsey's voice — very serious. What were you all on about?' I told her and said 'There's a legend about druids in Marton, you know. Shall we go mad and get Camembert *and* Stilton?'

'Temptation', I said 'that's what we were talking about.' On the way home we realized we had forgotten to buy bread. Barbara said she knew a home bakery where they did nice farmhouse loaves and their own French sticks.

'Just pull in here and I'll hop out.'

I said, 'But don't be long. It's a double yellow line.' I watched in the mirror as she joined the long queue. After a few minutes I also noticed in the mirror the traffic warden on my side of the road. He was walking slowly, but his pace had that inevitability about it which convinced me I was predestined to receive a ticket. I sat staring unseeing at the morning paper as I heard his cheerful whistling. It is hard to pretend nonchalance. He stopped two cars behind and seemed to be writing something on his pad. Seconds later he stuck his smiling face in at my window. I launched into a bluster of excuses. He nodded, not unsympathetically, I thought. Then, seeing my dog-collar, he said, with extravagant solemnity, 'Lead us not into temptation!' He walked off grinning and wagging his finger.

When Barbara came back she said, 'What did he give you? Did he give you anything?'

'Only a sermon,' I said. 'We do not live by bread alone.'

15

JUBILEE

There is much simple and sincere patriotism in the country-side and I think this is at least partly due to the fact that this land, England, is so much more visible and tangible in the country than it is in the towns. To see Wilf Johnson's corn standing in stacks in the fields on a sunny August evening is to get some gist of what poets have meant by the word 'England'. And to see the meadow by the river all overhung in a morning mist, with the lark singing, out of sight but clear and strong, is to enter a communion which is, to say the least, rather more encouraging than that evoked by the fog and drizzle of the industrial towns. But I will not deny that countryfolk are less sophisticated than the townspeople and that they have fewer problems as a consequence. This also contributes to a tradition which is at once conservative and royalist as well as patriotic. So, when plans for the Queen's Jubilee were announced, Marton like most villages set itself to make a splash.

There was a preliminary meeting in the village hall to sketch out general plans. Chairs had been put out in circular formation and I guessed that this must have been the work of Jonathon ('Jonty') Clayton, the sociology lecturer who had come to live in Marton West Grange. Jonty was widely regarded as a man of intelligence and imagination and he was a creative force in many village organizations from the PTA to the Thursday night badminton club. His wife Astrid worked with clay and ran the yoga class.

When I arrived the hall was already half full. There was a

cheerful mumbling of greetings and suggestions, remembrances of royal events past, and of dutiful reference to the weather. As latecomers were obliged to clamber over the feet of those already settled, it was obvious that the price we paid for our 'restructured non-hierarchical open-ended seating pattern' was a few ladies' corns stepped upon by the heavy farmers.

Jonty bounded into the circle at just on eight o'clock. He was a handsome fellow with a neatly trimmed beard and he wore those special glasses which adjust themselves to the light, the lenses always a little on the dark side. In the bright evening sunlight which slanted across the room from the high windows, Jonty's eyes were quite invisible. 'Hi, folks!' he said, pacing about the middle of the ring like a trainer of wild animals. Alec Dunderdale, the big farmer from Top o' th' Brow, stood beside him looking shy; in wide-checked suit and waistcoat, he made an unlikely lion. Jonty performed for both of them. 'Alec and I, representatives of both Old Marton and New Marton, as you might say, would like to welcome you to this first meeting of the village Jubilee project.' He had a habit of tapping his foot as he spoke, as if in time to popular music audible only to himself. He spoke only briefly before calling for ideas and suggestions from the floor 'because this Jubilee thing has got to be one great democratic thing.'

Mrs Baxter, sitting on the front row in her hair-net and old wellington boots, said we should 'do as we did before'. The trouble with this suggestion was that not everyone's memory stretched back as far as the 1930s. Jonty himself, forty odd years ago, had not been so much as a pinprick on a demographer's chart. Tins of toffees, mugs with their names on, bunting in the village street, a service of commemoration in the parish church — all these things were decided upon just as they had been almost half a century ago. Saville, huge and immaculate, in a voice which always sounded closer to song than to speech, said he had a great vision of Marton on the day 'as a place of lights and music and dancing, where the arts and skills of the inhabitants should all combine to produce a festival of all the talents that would be remembered for ever.' He made it sound like nothing less than that Great and notable Day of the Lord, so long expected yet so long delayed. The locals eyed one another knowingly as Saville spoke — like companions in the front stalls signalling that they had rumbled the plot. Their grins widened as Jonty clapped his hands and told the iridescent Saville that Astrid would be most enthusiastic about supervising anything on the arts and crafts side. Alec Dunderdale looked a bit like a clown in that loud check suit but he spoke like the straight man: 'We don't want to get too many fancy ideas into our heads — I mean overstretching ourselves. It's one thing talking about what you're going to do, and it's another thing paying for it.' Loud cries of 'Hear! Hear!' from the floor.

Miss Martindale sat on the raised bench under the window. She looked like a bird of prey on a high perch — she pounced, chirruping: 'It's all right for such as Mr Saville talking big. But we haven't all got posh estate agents' offices in Leeds — and the brass that goes with it.' She nodded sharply then turned her head to one side as if she had no more interest in the meeting and had decided to carry out a minute inspection of the wallpaper.

'I'm not talking about a lot of expense,' said Julian Saville reassuringly, 'but about the people of Marton letting the world see they know how to set about these things. Putting ourselves on the map, you know. Showing our metal — that sort of thing'. He smiled and sat down. Up sprang Miss Martindale again, her shrill voice sounding even fiercer after Saville's mellifluous tones: 'But the world won't be watching, will it Mr Saville? The world will be having its own jubilee party — it won't be taking any notice of what's going on in Marton.'

Saville stood up and smiled even more genially than before. 'I was merely being metaphorical.' He made a gesture as if sweeping the dust off his chair then sat down again. The old villagers distrusted metaphors almost as much as they distrusted posh businessmen who had their offices in the city and came to live in the best houses in Marton. At that moment they would have settled for toffees and mugs, for a bit of bunting and a patriotic anthem from the choir at Evensong as a perfectly adequate commemoration of the Jubilee. It was Jonty Clayton who prevented the springs of imagination drying up altogether.

'You said the word Miss Martindale — a party. That's what we must have, a jubilee party for the whole village!'

'A party?' Miss Martindale's mouth turned the shape of a dried fruit. She pronounced the word 'party' as if it was another word for 'sin'. She continued, 'And just what sort of party were you thinking of, Mr Clayton?'

'As I said, Miss Martindale, one for all the village.'

She replied in rapid speech, her voice on a monotone. It was as if she were making a catalogue of Clayton's crimes: 'Not a party in the style of Marton annual barbecue, I hope — Mr Bennington's barn taken over by the licensee of the village inn and that dreadful, loud music booming until the small hours, the foul language, the noise and the stench of motor bikes, the streets left filthy . . .'

Jonty Clayton glanced sharply at her and his dark glasses looked black as a mask in the last of the autumn sunshine. 'We all know about your disapproval of our biggest annual fund-raising event, Miss Martindale.'

'It's not the fund-raising I disapprove of but the noise, the hooliganism, the squalor . . .'

Now it is a rare thing for a clergyman to be able to point to any single good he has achieved, but I think some lucky star must have been shining as I stood up and said, 'If it's a parish party we're planning, we should use the new school.' Silence.

The effect lay in the nature of the building itself rather than in any fatherly authority of mine. People valued the new school — it would not be going too far to say they even respected it. So while the bourgoisie of Marton and their guests from the fleshpots of Leeds and York might think nothing of using Bennington's barn as a venue for their intoxicated intimacies and annual rowdiness, they would surely behave with more discretion in the school for fear of the PTA if nothing else.

'The Vicar's right!' said Alec Dunderdale. There was murmured agreement. I was stunned by such rare approbation. Miss Martindale seemed stunned too. She stood as if she meant to make another of her denunciations, then she sniffed loudly and made towards the door, not without difficulty as she stumbled over the circle of legs which was the result of Clayton's radical seating plan.

'You've done it now, Vicar. You've gone and offended Miss Martindale.' And I saw the success of my earlier diplomacy evaporate before my eyes.

The rest of the evening was given to forming a committee to look after the detailed planning. They were set on a party, Miss Martindale's dyspepsia notwithstanding. Alec Dunderdale came across and breathed pipe smoke and commiseration: 'She'll come round, Vicar. You know what she's like. It wasn't your fault, now. Everybody wants a party.'

'Except Pussy Puritan! Who does she think she is standing in judgement? What's it got to do with her how people enjoy themselves?' Astrid Clayton stood beside me, simmering in the full heat of her indignation. Jonty came across and put his hand on her shoulder. 'Don't be uptight, 'Strid. As Alec says, the old bird will come round.' The yoga teacher had flailed about like a manic semaphorist under her kaftan, but she was soothed by Jonty's reassurance and ran off into the far corner where a small group of playgroup mothers were thinking about a beautiful baby competition for the afternoon of the festival.

Suddenly it was all taking shape according to the principle of disciplined chaos which always seems to bring the appearance of order to village events. Dunderdale stood in the middle of the room taking a note of the various ideas and suggestions which folk mentioned on their way out. He was like a huge centripetal force drawing all the whirling bits and pieces to himself. During the following few weeks he would visit the people whose names he now scribbled in the margin of last month's copy of *Farmer and Grower*, and he would get them to translate vague promises into tangible effects — effects as various as a vegetable show, children's sports, fancy dress, country dancing, cream teas, car-park attending and the raffle. In this task he would be abetted by all the forces of Leeds Polytechnic — or at least by those of them susceptible to the influence of senior lecturer Clayton, whose special interests were the sociology of Max Weber and the organising of village fêtes. As for me, I knew I must go round and visit Miss Martindale.

The next day I arrived to find her at her sewing by the window. Her hair was whiter than the white lace curtains. As she bent forward abruptly to snap the cotton in her teeth, she seemed more than ever like a bird of prey. I tapped gently on the low window. She turned sharply, ready to frown on some new nuisance, put down her work on a large platter in the window and came to let me in — no swift task given the number and stiffness of bolts, locks and chains on the door of the old cottage.

'Good afternoon, Miss Martindale.'

'You can't be too careful. That's why I keep it on the lock. Mrs Edgeworth near the Post Office was broken into the other week. That's the way of the world today.' As she spoke, the door was still not fully opened and her words seemed to be a way of gaining time until she made quite certain that I was who I appeared to be and not some outrageously disguised vandal come to terrorise her under the cover of the Lord.

'You'd better come in.'

The cottage was as small and neat as Miss Martindale herself. It darkened considerably as she shut the door behind us. She gave the discarded sewing a stare as if daring it to move from where it had been ceremoniously placed. There was a vaguely clinical aroma — mothballs, eucalyptus or the like — which seemed to go well with the brilliant white of the cloths covering the small table and the backs of the chairs.

'I must tell you, I cannot abide that Mr Clayton with his silly spectacles and his even sillier ideas. As for his wife . . . and the beard.'

'I didn't think Mrs Clayton had a beard.'

Emily Martindale, who if the truth be told was not without the hint of a beard herself, shrugged in exasperation and pulled her cardigan tightly round her shoulders. She spoke more calmly: 'I was just making a little dress for my god-daughter.'

The words were a way of apologizing for her uncharitable outburst against the sociology lecturer.

'And how are they getting on, your god-daughter and her mother?'

A yellow lorry squealed to a standstill outside the store opposite and Miss Martindale peered round the lace curtains

at the delivery man whistling in and out of Grant's with
new-baked loaves. She answered without turning round.

'It's not often I hear from them these days. She never
even acknowledged her birthday card. I sent little Claire
some socks — two pairs — but I heard nothing.'

'She must be growing up.'

'She'll be three in March. She was always round here as a
baby when they lived in Marton. Her mother used to put
the carry-cot across the chair where you're sitting. We'd chat
all afternoon while Claire slept. We were such good friends.
Music, you know. Annnabelle played the violin and it was a
chance remark in the store one day led to her coming across
to look at my collection. People used to think we were
mother and daughter. Then her husband got promotion
and they moved to Bristol. Well, you know all about it.' The
lorry gave a great sneeze and spluttered off round the
corner. She added, 'I don't suppose I'll see them again.
You'll have a cup of tea while you're here?'

'When you send the little dress, I'll give you a handbill to
put in the parcel — about the Jubilee.'

One minute she was standing in the kitchen door with
the tea caddy in her hand and looking like a sentimental
portrait of an old lady; next minute she was bustling about
the place, her movements brisk with exaggerated exactness,
her speech a long chant of indignation:

'I'd rather hear no more about the Jubilee if you don't
mind. That's why you've come isn't it, the reason for your
calling — to soothe me with sweet talk after I walked out of
that dreadful meeting? Well, I won't be soothed! Do you
hear?'

There was a silence and she leaned forward against the
sink, her head bowed, her hand tightly gripping the kettle. I
saw she was weeping. The tears came quietly at first and her
face went through many contortions in the attempt to blink

them back. Then she began to sob, breaking off now and
then to excuse herself: she was a silly old woman; I was to
take no notice; she'd get a grip of herself in a minute, and so
on.

Soon we sat opposite each other at the small table and
sipped our tea. Her red eyes looked narrow and tired. She
could have done with Jonty's dimmer specs. I put another
sugar lump on my spoon and watched it dissolve just under
the surface of the strong tea. Miss Martindale dabbed at her
face and sniffed. 'I'm sorry, Vicar. I do apologize. Making a
fool of myself like that. I don't know what came over me.'

Then it all came out. She had become so attached to
Annabelle and little Claire that she had felt deserted when
they left. 'Some days, if I've nothing to go over to Grants'
for, I don't speak to a soul all day. I sit in the window and
watch them all going by. And I sew — but that doesn't do
any good either. Then I get so I can't sleep at night. And you
imagine all sorts. And get up, and make endless cups of tea.
And the house seems cold. I never used to mind about
living alone but now . . . I don't know . . . it's having no one
to talk to. When they started talking about parties the other
night, well, I felt so horrible, so left out. And now I'm
disgusted with myself.'

'Stop being disgusted and pour some more tea please.'

The following week I called again, with the handbill
about the Jubilee. We drank more tea. I said, 'You know
you're quite good at this tea-making business. Why don't
you stroll on to the school one of these afternoons? They
have a cuppa in the staffroom at about half-past two. I took
the liberty of telling Mrs Tate about your collection of
violins. She'd love the children to see them.'

It was a success from the beginning — not just the
exhibition of Miss Martindale's fiddles but the sewing class

that she began for the Upper Juniors. And when the day of the Jubilee celebrations arrived, one of the most popular stalls at the school's display was that containing the needlework of the girls (and the boys) from the top class. There was a party, of course; in fact there were several. Miss Martindale sat in a quiet corner with Mrs Tate, Miss Riley and Alec Dunderdale and his wife. Jonty Clayton was doing the announcing for the dancers. Emily Martindale did not dance but late in the evening Jonty went across to her table, bent conspiratorially between Emily and Miss Riley and soon they were all laughing. From where I was sitting at the other side of the room, this was all a mime and I do not know what was actually said. But I saw Jonty returning to his microphone, a broad smile sandwiched between the beard and the dimmers, and the next minute a movement of white hair in the shadows as Miss Martindale stood with the others for the anthem and goodnight.

16

THREE SCORE YEARS AND . . .

The Church of England is marginally less generous than the Lord in the matter of the span which it allows its servants: whereas the divine counsel grants three score years and ten, the Church requires its clergy to retire at the age of sixty-eight. Most parsons are glad to retire, to stow their surplices (or whatever other expression might be the ecclesiastical equivalent of the footballer's hanging up his boots) and to take a back pew in their declining years, to exchange the draughty vicarage and the insistent telephone for the comfortable anonymity of a retirement bungalow on the edge of the country. So the approach of the sixty-eighth year becomes a time for the rehearsal of valedictory sermons and for digging out St. Paul's famous text of self-congratulation: 'I have run the race . . . I have kept the faith, etc.'

Not so with Harry Lodge, MSc, BD, of the parish of Clough, eight miles from Marton. The rural Dean took him on one side at the end of the last chapter meeting: 'How long have you got now, Harry?'

There followed a loud expostulation from the corner as if the two men were two ladies coming suddenly across a mouse. Harry's penetrating voice was a mixture of stentorian indignation and injured innocence: 'How long have I got? As long as the good Lord chooses to spare me; that's how long I've got.' Burly Harry stood his ground and looked so ferociously at his brother clergyman that he might have been an old sea dog preparing to repel boarders. The Rural Dean reminded him of the Sixty-Eight Rule.

'Aye but they can't have me on that, old boy. There's a qualification to that rule . . .' He held his large hand a few inches from his face and stared into it as if he were reading the qualification from his palm. '. . . anyone who was inducted to his living before the Sixty-Eight Rule was passed in 1976 is not governed by the rule. I've been in Clough since '65, old boy. So they can't lay a finger on me.' He slapped his leg loudly and set his face in motionless defiance.

Harry Lodge was a large man in every sense of the word. His face wore a countryman's complexion and great black thickets of eyebrows — a touch of super-realism under his fine silvery hair. He despised the motor car along with most of the modern world and its trappings. He walked everywhere — meaning to his vicarage, the fourteenth-century parish church on the hill, the private houses of his parishioners and the public house in Clough — with long strides that made his progress appear inexorable. He always carried a stick and, except in the very hottest weather, he wore his old-fashioned three-quarter coat. He was, too, in every sense of the word, a gentleman. The loud voice could drop to a whisper and still be heard at the back of a crowded church. To see him at a baptism made you think he would have been excellent as a children's nurse. And with the old folk — some old folk younger than himself — he was a great favourite on account of his patience and his ready ear.

Harry's routine never varied: up at six-thirty and out down the lane with the dog; a cup of tea and a slice of toast by the stove in the old kitchen; across to church at eight for Morning Prayer; letters (which he hated) followed by milky coffee (which he loved); an hour, as he said, 'encouraging the weeds' in his garden; lunch; visiting in the parish from two until half-past four; a bath in place of tea — no vicar with half an eye on his waistline takes afternoon tea, since his inside will be awash already with the offerings of the folk he was called upon; Evening Prayer at six and, if there was no council meeting, confirmation class or the like he would take his supper and his ale together at 'The Woodman' in Clough.

Dolly Ackroyd at 'The Woodman' liked to fuss over him. He usually left the pub at a quarter past ten and it was then that visitors to the parish would look up from their pints and pass some remarks about the parson's presence in the bar. Dolly would tell them: 'That's Mr Lodge, our vicar. He comes in here religiously.' She would pronounce that last word with solemn emphasis then turn to the mirror under the optics and scan her make-up. Like many of the parishioners, Dolly would lose no opportunity to refer to the vicar's MSc degree, speaking reverentially to visiting sceptics or potential critics and saying, 'He's a Master of Science you know.' For Dolly and the others, Harry's qualification in science put him in the mystical category, as if a parson versed in secular understanding must know things hidden from ordinary mortals. Though sometimes, even this accolade could turn into a backhanded compliment — as when Dolly, towards the end of some long summer evening, would lean, all mellow and sentimental, across the bar and whisper, 'You know Harry, you could have gone a long way with your science.'

Harry would smile distantly and say that he did not want to go a long way: 'The Woodman' at Clough was far enough for him.

There was another person in Clough who had reason to be glad of Harry's scientific training: Mark Dunderdale, headmaster of the village school. One morning about five years ago he had grabbed Harry's sleeve on the way out of prayers and ushered him into the office. 'Thing is, Mr

Lodge, the local authority advisers are going a bomb on this "Science in the Junior School" idea. There's been an official report about it — I expect you've heard — and the government is pushing like mad. Well, we've no one in Clough Juniors well up enough in science to push back. I wondered if you would like to come in one morning a week and teach the rudiments to the top class? 'Course, I know you're very busy.'

'I'd be delighted, if you thought I'd be any use.' The black eyebrows were raised until they almost touched the silvery hair. Harry was thinking to escape the letters and the weeding; he knew his milky coffee was safe in the staffroom at break.

The children in class five came to like him. They called him 'The Minstrel' on account of his forgetfulness which had caused him, two weeks running, to repeat his loud and atmospheric recitation of an extract from *The Lay of the Last Minstrel*. Moreover, it was the sort of science that bordered on the miraculous: beakers of various dilute acids and alkalis changed colour and even turned back into clear liquids in the vicar's demonstration. In his white coat and dog-collar he stood like a wizard at the front of the class, juggling test tubes and glass jars over the bunsen burner and explaining oxygen, nitrogen and the rest as if he were master of the elemental spirits. He was like a grandfather to the children, and the teaching offered a small but welcome augmentation to the stipend.

On one of the mornings when he did not teach, Harry went to pick up his letters from the mat as usual. There was a large brown envelope from the diocesan office and marked 'Confidential'. It contained a letter from the Secretary (Parishes) and a wad of glossy publications from the church commissioners on the subject of 'Clergyman and Retirement'. There were pictures of frail parsons standing outside chalets that looked as if they had been hastily built in some utility Nirvana. There were prominently daubed rhetorical questions like 'Where do I go from here?' and 'What does it cost?' There were pages of accounts 'for example', setting out the Commissioners' low interest mortgage scheme. But it was the letter from the Secretary (Parishes) which drew the vicar's attention. It was written in the style of the comradely coercive as from one brother in Christ evicting another from his last staging post:

'Dear Brother,

    Retirement can be an anxious time for the parochial clergyman accustomed as he is to his freedom and independence. This letter is an attempt, on behalf of the Diocesan Ministry Committee, to minimize the disturbing effects of the retirement process. The various enclosures explain the possibilities of the situation with regard to housing provision and include facts, figures and examples to help you decide on which particular scheme is the most appropriate in your own case.

    I should add that I am available, in my capacity of Secretary for Parishes, to discuss any or all of these arrangements — or indeed any other matters in any way connected with them. If you feel you would like a private meeting, please telephone me at this office. Your retirement date is scheduled 30.9.84.

Yours sincerely,
J.E.Wilderspool'

It was Canon Wilderspool in one of his many administrative disguises. Harry's immediate reaction was to pick up the telephone and explain curtly that he had no intention of retiring. As he sat by the hall table, his pulse pounding under his stock, his eyes roaming over the pictures of the Nirvana chalets, he framed and reframed his opening gambit to the authorities. But the telephone only continued the ringing tones for so long that Harry conjectured the staff of the diocesan office must themselves have retired en bloc. At last he put down the telephone and the garish literature and sat in silence staring through the door's frosted glass at the distorted movements of light and shade in the garden. The origin of these movements was the approach of a visitor up the long drive. It was Dolly from 'The Woodman'.

'I just came to say that Eric and me's going off for a few days — he's sick of being tied to the pub. Anyhow, there's a nice couple — Vernon and Enid — coming from the brewery, and I just wanted you to know that Enid'll have your supper ready at the usual time.' She fussed fastidiously over a turned-up piece of carpet next to the doormat. Harry did not move. She looked at him acutely as if his silence had been an interruption. 'Hey, what's the matter? Are you not so well — or has somebody been upsetting you, or what?'

He glanced involuntarily at the pile of papers by the telephone. Her eyes followed his movement. In a quiet voice she said, 'It's not bad news, I hope.'

He stood up and forced his huge face to stretch into a phoney smile. 'No, it's not bad news. Just Anno Domini you know. Every dog has its day and all good things come to an end, eh?'

She looked puzzled. In a movement that was half like a man swatting a fly and half like the same man blessing a crowd, he laid a hand on her shoulder. 'They say I must retire, Dolly. They think you're past it when you're sixty-eight.'

His other hand flicked over the pile of papers, and pictures of happy retired clergy peered up at Dolly Ackroyd from among the sunlit chalets.

'Retire?' She sounded as shocked as she had been that day when Don Carter the blacksmith had come into 'The Woodman' and ordered himself a bitter lemon. 'You can't retire. What would you do? What would *we* do?'

He paced slowly up and down the hall. 'You would get a new vicar and I would go and live in one of those.' He glared at the coloured brochure.

'But you can't live in a place like that. It's like a Butlin's holiday camp.' She picked up the brochure and eyed it disdainfully. 'Besides, look at the creepy characters who live there — they look as if half a pint of Eric's bitter would knock 'em flat!' He looked at the awful picture and knew what she meant. There was a pause, then Dolly said the one word, 'When?'

'Oh, not for some time yet. And in any case they can't force me to retire. But it's the official policy — out at sixty-eight — and so they'll do everything in their power.'

'And how long's "some time"?'

'Not until the end of September.' He tried to sound nonchalant.

She was aghast. She held a hand before her face and began to count on her fingers: 'September — that's only one-two-three-four . . . *five* months!'

'There's all the summer to be got through first.'

'Summer! And how long's summer in this country? Humph! Well, I'm not going to stand idly by, I can tell you. We'll get up a petition. I'll . . .'

He smiled a natural smile and laid both hands on her shoulders. 'Dolly, I know you mean every word. But this is not something to be settled by letters and petitions. It's up to me. I have to decide whether I'm going to take a stand against standard practice, that's all. I'd be within my rights but there would be a lot of fuss. They wouldn't want to think I was setting a trend — encouraging other parsons to be bolshy.'

He asked her if she would like a cup of coffee made with milk and they sat for half an hour and looked out over the garden which was fresh and iridescent after the early morning rain. Eventually, Dolly said she would have to be going to do the lunches. Eric would be all on his own. He opened the front door and watched as she strode jauntily towards the gate. She turned and waved. The sneck clicked and he was alone with his threatened freehold.

Over the following few weeks Harry phoned a couple of times about deanery affairs and it occurred to me to ask whether he had made up his mind about retirement.

'I've decided to go, Peter.' Silence while I wondered what to say next.

'But they can't make you, Harry. You were in Clough before 1976.'

'Oh, I know. That's what I told the Rural Dean. But I've no stomach for a fight. And I wouldn't like to end my time at Clough on a sour note. It would only queer the pitch for my successor. I know the rules, though: the only thing they can get an incumbent out for — excluding his absence from the parish for more than three months at a stretch — is if they can prove he's an open and notorious evil liver. My liver must be pretty evil after all these years — but it's not notoriously so.'

At the end of June, Clough Juniors put on a carnival to mark the school's centenary. It happened that Canon Wilderspool — in another of his incarnations as Chairman of the Diocesan Education Committee — was invited. In the morning he had presided at a special service of thanksgiving in Harry's church. The afternoon was spent in sports, sideshows and a sale of work, after which the children were put to bed and their parents came out for the centenary dinner and dance in the school hall.

It was a calm, humid evening after a very warm day, and there was still plenty of light in the sky at half-past ten. The wide windows of the hall had been folded back and guests sat out on the porch between the main building and the playing fields. Dances alternated between easy-beat slouches to suit the middling exhausted middle-aged, and the brassy freneticism of hot rock for the more virile members of the PTA. The Canon danced a foxtrot with the headteacher's wife. Mark Dunderdale sat alone at his table for the duration of this ghostly phenomenon. When the agile Canon returned the lady to her white wine and stuffed olives, the two men walked out together on to the porch where they were seen to be engaged in enthusiastic conversation for almost an hour. That was a Saturday night. The next Tuesday morning Harry received a further letter from the Secretary (Parishes). It was, as they say, 'personalized'.

'My dear Harry,

As you will be aware, we have been processing the documentation of your retirement in accordance with section 5(e) ix of Diocesan Regulations p. 439 ff *Incumbents Retirement Measure* (1976 revised). Under the terms of that measure provision is made (under *Special Circumstances*, paras (f), (h) and (j) p. 445) for certain exclusions and for cases where alternative arrangements can sometimes be made.

Mr Mark Dunderdale, head-teacher of Clough C. of E. Juniors, on behalf of his board of governors (and after representing them at an Extraordinary Meeting in your absence) has written to express their fears that your retirement would have an unfortunate effect on the science policy of the school. He supports his board's views with a letter from the County Science Adviser, Mr I. Patrington.

Accordingly (under section J(ii) on p. 445) I am writing to ask whether, in the special circumstances, you would be prepared to defer your retirement from the benefice of St Andrew's, Clough until such time as shall be agreed as mutually convenient.

Yours as ever,
John E. Wilderspool'

Harry went into school as usual next morning. He was met by the anxious face and piping voice of Shane Eagleton at the front of class five: 'Is it true that you're retiring, Mr Lodge?'

'No Shane, it most certainly is not. Now, kindly deliver this note to Mr Dunderdale.'

It was a request to see the headteacher in his study at the end of the morning. At five minutes past twelve, the two men sat opposite each other in the strange quietness that is the aftermath of vanished children.

'I had no idea you were intending to do anything to stave off the inevitable. I was going to tell you my retiring date soon after the carnival.'

'You were pipped at the post, Harry'. The tall, wiry headteacher offered the Vicar a cigar. 'You of all people ought to know there are no secrets in villages. My Miss Hardy and Mr Turnbull are rather fond of popping into 'The Woodman' for a sandwich and a glass on Friday lunchtime. Mrs Ackroyd just happened to mention. . . .' The Vicar ran his fingers through the sparse silvery hair, then he lit the cigar and settled back in his armchair under a thickening cloud of aromatic smoke.

17

STRANGE THINGS FOR BREAKFAST

Before a vicar becomes a vicar he must spend some time as a curate. This gives him the chance to learn the trade and, if he is as fortunate as I was, to have a more experienced clergyman cover his worst mistakes. My first vicar was a Yorkshireman who, if not without guile, was certainly without the sort of affectation and the habits of circumlocution which north country folk associate with those who live further south. Harry Greensmith was blunt. He was small, almost squat, though by no means undernourished. He was the most alert person I have ever met. His very lived-in face generally wore an expression of genial scepticism as if he were always half-expecting someone to try and play a trick on him. He was opposed to all theories on principle. Life was a living thing to Harry Greensmith, a matter of visible, tangible effects that could be ordered in a practical down-to-earth way. He would struggle to change all those things that needed changing, and to leave unchanged all that was beyond change: moreover, he was wise enough to know the difference between them.

He was a conservative — not in the sense of having a particular philosophy; philosophy was only a theory and so it was outlawed by his general ban on things so tenuous. He believed in preserving what was good and he understood what at the time I did not understand: that the key to our interpretation of the present is always the heritage of formed ideas and experiences from the past.

I can remember sitting opposite him in Monday morning staff meetings, cups of milky coffee at our elbows, parson's pocket books on our knees. There were two of us, curates, minds filled with ideas that were only fairly adjacent to reality. Harry would tell us when we were to preach, how long, how loud and what about. He would ask for a list of the parishioners we had visited during the previous month. He would give instructions as to which one of us was to 'look in' on the Guides, Brownies, Scouts, Cubs, Mothers' Union, Young Wives and the Youth Club. Only then would he sit back in his leather chair, his lips curled sceptically round the end of his pen, one eye narrowing until it almost closed — as if he could see much more that way: 'Well, now, what have you got for *me*?'

What we had for him was some bright new scheme by which we hoped to bring enlightenment to the fusty folk of our congregation whom we perceived as wandering aimlessly in untheoretical darkness. 'We'd like to show a film about the work of the new liturgical movement.'

'What for?'

We had imagined the reason to be self-evident.

'It's just that modern services are more relevant to those not used to Church.'

'More relevant than what?'

'Well, the old Prayer Book, the Authorized Version.'

'But if they don't come to church (What did you say? — "aren't used to it") *all* forms of service will be equally irrelevant.'

'Why not let them hear the best?'

We made the mistake of thinking that 'the best' was a matter of opinion. Any attempted refutation of our half-formed notions would have seemed to Harry to take him too far into the nebulous realms of theory, so instead he offered earthier objections: 'You'll never get 'em to a film-show this time o' t' year. Too hot. Light nights. They want to be out in their gardens. Wait 'til it gets towards back end.'

He knew that, when autumn came people would be involved in far too many routine parish meetings to be able to spare any time for something as rarefied as the new liturgical antics.

Harry had no sympathy with things as contrived and derivative as films about worship, pamphlets on the Prayer Book and so on. Why have something that was only *about* a thing when you could with less effort have the thing itself? There was no need to fill life with articulate apologies and explanations; just get on with the job of living. Going to church was part of that job. It was simply what you *did*, what people had done for hundreds of years. No need to rationalize churchgoing; only *go* and the value of going would become obvious. O taste and see . . . what *else* was there to do? All those two years, even as I wriggled in exasperation on Greensmith's sofa, I was learning the reality of the parson's job as opposed to the wonderful apparitions of it that I had brought from the theological college. I did not, could not, acknowledge this at the time. Harry Greensmith gave me few formal lessons but I learned more from him than from anyone else; his ordinary words and movements were themselves the lessons, as an icon partly embodies the reality to which it points, as a Chinese character is a picture of the object which it names.

It was Harry who drove me to my first bishop's breakfast — a treat for all the parish clergy laid on by the Bishop of Ripon every year in the spring. We drove up from Leeds in a storm that was too much for the windscreen wipers. It was as if we were under water. Harry made comments on landmarks in the blurred countryside as we raced past them. He seemed to know something about every large house, every parish church, vicarage and motel along that whole stretch of the A1.

Before breakfast there was Holy Communion in the

cathedral. The space in front of the west door was packed
with damp, flustered clergy rushing to divest themselves of
mackintoshes and put on their surplices. There was the
usual banter: mumbling, chuckling parsons awash in small
talk about the weather. Occasionally, a loud, stylized clerical
voice would be heard shouting above the general din: this
was the Bishop's chaplain giving instructions about car-
parking and telling us where to find 'The White Rose Café'.
At nine o'clock we dawdled in a long procession to our
places in the chancel.

The Bishop was a small man with a big brain. He preached
in a thin staccato voice about St Francis of Assisi. As we
came down from Communion, watery sunlight moved
rapidly across the tracery on the north wall like someone
turning a page. All those male voices singing 'Forth in Thy
name O Lord I go' and we were out again on the windy west
front. A great crocodile of clergy set out for the café in the
market place. We were shown into a large, rectangular room
with a wide archway at one end so that it almost felt like
going back into church. It was deliciously warm and soft
after the cold stone of the cathedral, with an aroma of bacon
and eggs that was so strong it made you feel dizzy. The
Bishop shook hands with us all as we entered and his thin
voice through his thin smile could be heard making polite
enquiries about the parishes. Then he turned and went
towards the top table where he said a brisk Latin grace and
we fell upon the bowls of cornflakes.

Harry and I sat opposite Clive Martin, vicar of a country
parish on the Leyburn road, and Paul Sturrock who taught
theology in the University of Leeds. Sturrock had Rice
Crispies stuck in his ginger moustache. In a light, playful
voice he said, 'Does Harry Greensmith leave you any time
for reading, Peter?'

'Only *The Dandy*', said Harry without looking up.

There was a sharp hammering of a spoon on the table as if in comment on Harry's joke, and the booming voice of the Bishop's Chaplain solemnly announced the number of a motor car that had been parked where it ought not to have been. An embarrassed parson in a red muffler moved towards the door amid a shower of applause. The fried eggs were passed down the table as Sturrock said, '*The Dandy*, Harry! I thought you'd be reading *Radical Theology and the Death of God.*'

Harry handed Sturrock one of the hot plates. He said, 'I've no time to be reading fiction, Paul.'

There was a guffaw from Clive Martin.

'It's the coming thing, though,' said Sturrock quietly, persevering. 'The traditional stuff is definitely out, cuts no ice at all — like the old morality. Today's swingers have no time for GOD. All that sin, guilt and authority won't wash with the permissive society.'

'There's a few of your "permissive society" I've met who won't wash an' all', said Harry.

'Permissive society hasn't reached Leyburn deanery yet', said Clive Martin.

Harry mopped up some yolk with a crust of brown bread. 'It's all very well, your modern theology, Paul. But what's it got to do with ordinary folk in the parishes? They don't want it. Matter of fact they don't want theology of any sort: they want a church where they know the old routine still goes on — even though they don't go so often . . .'

'Oh yes, they like to know what they're staying away from!' said Sturrock.

'You can make fun if you like', said Harry. 'But what folks really want is a place where their kids can be baptized, a place to be wed — to be buried even. It's not theology. It's a sense of belonging.'

'But if the theoretical framework for your social activity is undermined by modern understanding — scientific progress — you can't just keep the show going as if nothing had happened. That would be hypocritical. Burying your head in the sand.'

Harry held his fork motionless before his mouth and stared unflinching at the theology teacher. 'I don't give tuppence for your "theoretical framework". It's the prayers themselves that provide the real framework. Are you trying to tell me that Ted Harrison's wanting to be buried in the corner of our churchyard is likely to be undermined by "scientific progress"?' He wiped the egg off his lips.

'No, but how many Ted Harrisons have you got? Not many, and they're getting scarcer — folks who'll believe what the parson says from the pulpit, who'll do as they're told. Today's generation — Bonhoeffer's "man come of age" — has no time for all that old authoritarian stuff.'

'So much the worse for them.'

'No, Harry! — so much the worse for you and your old church. The C of E is dying, Harry. It's already dead from the neck up.'

'What you're saying is that the worship and the way of going on which people have had in England for centuries must have been in some way wrong all the time — though *I* can't find much wrong with it. But what are you suggesting we change it for — for a few modern prejudices about what it's OK to believe and what it isn't? This "new understanding" and so called "liberation" that you and your friends spend all day talking about: it'll only become unfashionable soon and die off to be replaced by some other fad. But if in the meantime we use fashionable talk to talk the Church out of existence . . . what will we be left with then, eh?'

'You're an old stick-in-the-mud, Harry, and I don't suppose you'll ever change. But look around you: the church is changing fast, very fast.'

'Oh, we know that. It's all the talk in the newspapers and on the television: parsons falling over themselves in their rush to deny all the Christian doctrine they promised at their ordination they'd uphold. Do you still say the *Te Deum*, Paul? I don't suppose you do. But you remember where it says "the noble army of martyrs"? — what do you think those who died for their faith think of your modern lot who are busy handing the Church over to atheists and secularists?'

Sturrock looked genuinely hurt. 'But it's not faith we're chucking out, Harry — not faith as an authentic possibility, as a valid existential choice faced by each individual in his uniqueness — only the crumbling old words and doctrines in which faith has been so long imprisoned.'

Harry put down his knife and fork carefully, as if there were theological significance in their exact position on the cloth. He spoke quietly. 'But faith *is* those words, those doctrines. Take them away and what happens to faith? Well, it has to find some other words. And what does it find? It finds your words and those of your friends. And they're worse words, words not worth believing in, like "authentic possibility", "existential choice", "uniqueness" and all the rest. Well, Ted Harrison and all the Ted Harrisons that are still left — that will be here still when your bright modern church has come and gone — they've got some better words: better because they're simpler. Better because they're more solid, more homely: "Man that is born of woman . . .", "We do not presume . . .", "The peace which passeth understanding".'

Sturrock had finished his breakfast. He was piling up his plates and draining the dregs from his teacup. The man who had gone out to shift his car returned unapplauded. Sturrock said, 'We'll just have to wait and see. What I would say is this: The new Prayer Book will be out soon, and then there'll be no going back. And everywhere the trend is against you. You'll be forced to change or die.'

Harry muttered something under his breath. It sounded like 'the noble army of martyrs.' Then he stood up and said in a loud voice, 'Well, that'll be nowt fresh, Paul; the trend is always against us. "My Kingdom is not of this world" — remember!'

The Bishop got up and made a short speech followed by another brisk Latin prayer. I was wondering what trend *that* belonged to. We strolled out as we had strolled in. The sun shone brightly over the old town. The clock in the market square struck eleven. The narrow streets seemed littered with surfeited clergy. A little girl caught sight of us all. '*What* are *they*, Mummy?' she said. 'They look so strange!'

'Shh! They're the men who look after the churches, love.'

I was standing by the bookshop window. Harry Greensmith and Paul Sturrock shook hands and we walked off in opposite directions.

18

ALL SOUND AND FURY

Connie Hinchcliffe said at the church council meeting that it was time we celebrated the church's anniversary. 'I've an old watercolour of the day it was consecrated,' she said. 'Made me think it was time we remembered our origins. 'Course, things have changed a lot since those days.' And she floated off into a wistful reverie. I felt as if I could see her imagination printed on her eyelids: slim young ladies with long frocks and parasols; the Bishop's carriage and the Bishop himself about to put his foot on the kerb by the lychgate; the children; the quaint pepperpot tower and the new bells.

It had been one of those council meetings that drag on from one affair of petty finance to another. Talk of something that smacked of festivity came as a relief. There was a shuffle of movement around the table.

'What a good idea! Why don't we get the Bishop and a brass band?' said John Mason. I thought of a purple shirt and a pectoral cross heaving behind a euphonium.

'And bring in the Sunday school.'

'And the Scouts and Guides.'

'We could have a few stalls outside — you know, on the Saturday. Make a weekend of it.'

'Why not continue it with a flower festival?'

It was more interesting than talking about raising the cash to pay the diocesan quota. The treasurer frowned and said flowers were expensive. But Mrs Hinchcliffe was in full bloom. 'Nonsense, Michael. The stall and the collecting plate will more than offset the price of a few flowers.'

And so we appointed a steering committee, fixed the date

and I said I would write to the Bishop and ask him to come and preach. John Mason would ask the lads in the brass band when he joined them at their annual dinner in a couple of weeks' time. Mrs Taylor asked if she should bring Tessa the pony and charge twenty pence for rides. The treasurer wondered if that would mean we had to take out extra insurance: 'I heard of someone being kicked by a donkey at a village fair once.'

Mrs Taylor, who packed quite a kick herself, retorted, 'Kick? My Tessa wouldn't kick anyone. Wouldn't dream of it. And she is *not* a donkey!'

I pictured the sceptical treasurer on a dreaming donkey. Blessed is he that cometh in the name of the overdraft! Ten minutes later they all meandered out into the still warm evening, chattering about the anniversary. All except Walter Sykes. He remained lurking by the bay window and pretending to groom one of the overgrown house plants. He continued in this work as, without lifting his eyes, he said,

'They've all gone, the others then, Vicar?'

'Yes, you're the last, Walter.'

Then he did look up. 'Perhaps I can speak my mind, then, if you're sure there's only you and me?'

'Say on!' I affected what I hoped would be taken as genial nonchalance. But Walter Sykes fixed me with an unwavering look. He had a reputation and he knew that I knew he had a reputation — for putting a spanner in the works.

'You know what I think, Vicar?'

I had a pretty good idea.

'It's this anniversary lark . . .' he pronounced every syllable of the word with exaggerated deliberation. 'It's all sound and fury signifying nothing.' He seemed pleased with his phraseology.

'Well, I can't see how you make that out, Walter. I mean an anniversary is an anniversary. What it signifies is our gratitude for St Luke's over all these years.'

'Pah! Gratitude's misplaced. Your church'll be there when we've all gone. What do we want to remember it for? Michael was right when he said it would cost too much.'

'As far as I remember, he didn't say it would cost too much; he simply wondered at the price of flowers.'

'Same thing!'

'But you heard what Mrs Hinchcliffe said: the takings will pay for the flowers — easily.'

He walked away from the sickly plant as if he could do nothing to rescue it. 'Anyhow, it's not just money as I'm worried about. It's that, when you come to arranging big do's like this, it always falls on the same handful of folks to do all the donkey work. And when all's done, there's never the response you'd hoped for — not for putting in all that effort.'

Sykes was an old farmer not without his troubles. He had only recently lost his potato crop. As he himself said at the time: 'Guaranteed prices and compensation — well, it's all right I suppose, but it's no substitute for seeing them sacks on that lorry.' Besides it was well known that his two sons had no intention of following him into the business. His life's work had seemed to be for nothing. The farm would be sold when he died. It gave him a sense of failure, of disappointment as of a covenant unkept.

I said, 'Well, plenty of folk turned out for the Jubilee celebrations.'

'That's different.' He looked morose but he could not deny it. He took out his pocket watch and polished the face slowly on the leather patches of his sleeves. I went across and put my hand on his shoulder. 'Come on, Walter, you know it'll be fun when we all get going.'

'Fun? Some folks have got more important things to think about than fun.'

He looked tired, at the end of his tether. Everyone knew he was trying to hang on at the farm as long as possible, but he was seventy-two.

'How's the harvest coming along?'

He moped. 'Harvest? It's all right. Not this year's harvest I'm bothered about though, is it? How many more harvests am I going to see on Bridge Farm? That's what I'd like to know. I dun't like anniversaries.' he said, coming back suddenly to the point at issue, 'They remind me too sharply of how time's going.'

'I was hoping for your help, in particular — I mean, concerning the anniversary.'

His eyes flickered. Curiosity got the better of despair. ''Sort of help?'

'Etherington's model railway. If we're going to have a flower festival, we might as well have his steam engines in church. They're ever so popular.'

'I haven't seen Joshua Etherington for a long while.' He stared out of the window as if he were expecting to see Etherington on the lawn.

'I saw him the day before yesterday — in the hardware shop at Knaresborough. 'Course, we didn't know we were having a flower festival then. In any case, it would be better if *you* asked him.'

The tired face brightened. 'Well, I know Joshua's funny old ways better than most, I suppose. He doesn't mean any harm. He's not really used to seeing people. That's what it is that seems to make him a bit offhand like. But I've known him . . . must be forty years and more.'

'I know you have, Walter. That's why I'd like you . . .'

'D'you remember? — no, you won't remember, it was before you came —.' His face was mobile, illuminated with glee at his recollection, 'Silly old devil nearly burned his house down, mucking about with his engines. It was a

summer night — about this time of year. We were just
having a cup of cocoa. I said to Elsie, "There goes fire
engine. I bet it's old Brocklehurst's barn — he piles the straw
too high, too tight. I told him he was asking for trouble."
Anyhow, we stepped outside and there was this black smoke
coming down from old Joshua's. I jumped in the landrover
but when I arrived the firemen had it all under control. All
Joshua was worried about was his engines. Fireman said,
"We had to stop him running back in when the blaze was at
its worst."' He paused, then let out his breath in a series of
little sniffs and sniggers.

Walter agreed to see Etherington. Mrs Taylor agreed to
bring the non-donkey Tessa. Mason came to an agreement
with the boys in the band. Connie Hinchcliffe, by contrast,
was still quibbling with the florist over the price of blooms.
She telephoned to let off steam: 'I wouldn't mind, Vicar,
but I only want a few of the large blooms for the altar
display. I'm getting the rest free from local gardens. If Sarah
Carter thinks we can afford to spend a hundred pounds in
her florist's, she's got another think coming!' I looked after
posters and publicity. Old Sykes' words about 'there's never
the response' had goaded me into wanting to ensure a full
church.

It turned out to be a great success. Two days of unbroken
sunshine. Three coachloads of tourists from the Women's
Institute in Leeds. Plenty of nice publicity in *The York
Press*. And, of course, there were the cream teas. The band
played all Saturday afternoon — thirty of them, perspiring
foreheads in the heat, silvery instruments glinting in the
bright sunlight. In the evening there was a barbecue. All
weekend there was the chuff and clatter of Joshua
Etherington's model engines among the flowers. On Sunday
evening the Bishop came to preach and the church was full.
I managed a sly grin at Walter Sykes as he was handing out

the hymnbooks. Still he did not look very cheerful.

The next evening we had a meeting of the church council in the vicarage. 'Well, Mrs Taylor,' I said, 'Tessa didn't unseat anyone!'

Connie Hinchcliffe shook out her umbrella in the porch and scowled at the blackened sky. 'We just made it, eh Vicar? — one day to spare.' She was obviously pleased with herself. I was feeling rather pleased with myself too. Even the treasurer said everyone had enjoyed themselves. And the church had been full.

Then Walter Sykes spoke up. 'Well, Vicar, I'll tell you what I *didn't* like about last night's service . . .' There was a silence while he armed himself with a deep breath the better to fire his salvo. '. . . there weren't enough hymnbooks to go round, and I had to run across to fetch some from the Methodists. And their numbers are different to ours.' He looked very severe.

There was a pause for about five seconds that lasted three weeks. Then Walter's eyes flickered as they had when I first mentioned Etherington's railway. Connie Hinchcliffe could hardly stifle her laugh. I laughed. Then Walter laughed. He said, 'Take no notice of my grumbles. It's all sound and fury but it signifies nowt!'

When we had all finished laughing Walter added. 'And before we have the anniversary again next year, we ought to make sure the treasurer buys some more of the proper hymnbooks.'

19

A MODEST CELEBRATION

Mrs Walton wrote to me one Christmas to complain about the holding of the over-sixties Christmas party in 'The Acorn'.

'. . . and I have nothing against the landlord and his wife, selling drink to the public is, after all, his trade — though it is a trade for which I do not have a great deal of sympathy . . .' (That was putting it mildly!) '. . . but that the parish church should formally associate one of its organizations with a public house, I take to be an overstepping of the fine line which separates what is right and proper from what is not. It is the precedent I am thinking of, the example. Already certain members of the youth club frequent 'The Acorn', and I am regularly disturbed by them as they make their rather noisy way home at eleven o'clock at night. I feel that the moral basis for my complaints both at them and about them is being seriously undermined by the church's decision — whoever made the decision! — to engage the services of the inn and to advertise the fact in the parish magazine. Furthermore . . .'

There were two more pages of 'furthermore'. I decided the best thing would be for me to pay her a visit.

It was a bleak day in January. There was frost on the ground and a gale was blowing up, making the bare black branches on the trees in Church Lane thrash the air like whips. Mrs Walton lived in the cottage on the corner, between 'The Acorn' and the telephone box. 'If it's not rowdies tipping out of the public house, Vicar, it's vandals molesting the coin box. You would not like to live on this corner, I can tell you. It's like Bedlam.'

It was a roomy old cottage but the inside was fitted with all things new. Mrs Walton was a great one for gadgets: the knitting machine, the video recorder which was used only for tapes of opera and ballet taken from the television, the great variety of clocks and, sitting in the tiled hearth like some crazy piece of technologized Victoriana, her electric foot warmer. She pointed me towards a flimsy chair with stainless steel arms. It looked like an exhibit from the Institute for Contemporary Arts. It was surprisingly comfortable.

Annie Walton was a bright-eyed old puritan. With her sharpness, versatility and relentless energy she would have been a real asset on 'The Mayflower'. She was excessively thin through a combination of frugality and frenetic activity. She had short black hair and hollow cheeks, eyes blue and as electric as any of her gadgets. She offered me a cup of tea and, as if conceding my mortal failings, a small sugar bowl. Her own tea was taken without sugar or milk. She sat opposite me and smoothed her smock with her palms.

'It is kind of you to call in answer to my letter, Vicar.'

I stirred the silver spoon in my cup and remarked with as much unconcern as I could muster that sometimes events were taken out of context, mountains made out of molehills, wrong impressions were inadvertently given and so on.

'Oh, but not in this case, Vicar. The issue is quite clear!'

'But surely . . .'

'But surely, it cannot be right for the Church to be seen patronizing the public house?'

'Mrs Walton, there are public houses and then there are public houses. "The Acorn" is the village inn.'

'You don't need to remind me of that, Vicar. When my husband was alive, he spent more time "across the road" as he called it than ever he spent at home.'

'What I'm saying is that "The Acorn" — well, it's quite respectable!'

'Respectable!' she chirruped the word. 'Respectable is it now? Well, I'm not talking about respectability, Mr Mullen; I'm talking about sin.'

'That's usually my job!' The flippancy was a mistake.

'Indeed, Vicar. Indeed it is! And that's why I was so perplexed when I saw that you had given your backing to this . . . to these goings-on.'

'I'm sorry, Mrs Walton, but I just can't bring myself to think there's anything very sinful about the over-sixties popping in to "The Acorn" for a few mince pies and a glass of sherry.'

'"*Very* sinful" now is it? I'm sure you don't need reminding that sin is sin, Vicar; it is indivisible. Scripture says, "Wine is a mocker; strong drink is raging."'

'Indeed, Mrs Walton. And it also says "Take a little wine for your stomach's sake." St Paul himself, I believe.'

She was silent. Twigs from an overhanging tree beat against the window. It was overcast, sleeting. I walked over to the window and looked out on 'The Acorn'. It looked such an innocent place, the black and white of its neat paintwork and the curl of smoke from the bar chimney made it seem what in fact it was — a homely local alehouse. A voice from the avant-garde chair: 'Oh yes, it's all very quiet now. You come back at eleven o'clock tonight and it'll be quite a different story.'

'Mrs Walton, I'm sure you don't want to ban Christmas! That little outing was a treat for some of the old ones who live by themselves . . .'

'Many of us live by ourselves, Mr Mullen.'

'. . . it's not as if it's every week. It was a celebration, a very modest celebration, that's all.'

She began to clear away the tea things. It was time I went.

Suddenly the driving sleet burst into clear white snowflakes, huge and swirling, silent, creating the sensation that the whole street was floating through the air. 'The Acorn' looked like a chic Swiss chalet on a Christmas card.

'I wouldn't want you to go away without my having made myself quite plain, Mr Mullen.'

'Rest assured, you've certainly done that, Mrs Walton. And thank you for the tea. What kind was it, may I ask?'

She looked distracted for a moment, as if caught unawares. A touch of colour glowed in those hollow cheeks. 'Oh, it's nothing: a blend of China I'm rather fond of, that's all.'

'But you didn't get it from the village shop?'

'No, they don't have it there. I fetch it from Knaresborough.'

'Well, that's very nice — quite a treat, I think.'

She looked at the carpet and became very busy over a few crumbs.

I said, 'Look, I'll have a word with the youngsters about kicking up a din when they come out. But you know what youngsters are like . . .'

'Oh, I do! Indeed I do!'

'. . . well, we were all young once. I'll be going, Mrs Walton. Thanks very much for the tea — as I said, quite a little treat.'

I stepped into the street. The snow had fallen swiftly and the earth looked as pure and bright as Annie Walton's front room. I rushed past the shut and silent Acorn and arrived home just as the street lamps were coming on.

The next evening I went round to the pub after my confirmation class had finished at half-past nine. It was packed with youngsters. The new landlord and his wife were doing all they could to attract trade: there were baked potatoes and dishes of winter salad for the darts players; there were sausages on sticks and a tray of mince pies; there was also a shiny new jukebox which, however, was never played during a darts match. A few of the youth club were playing the fruit machine at the other end of the room. Sally, the landlord's wife, was behind the bar. Jim, her husband, was not in his usual place on the tall stool by the beer pumps.

I took my drink across to the squawking fruit machine. Jenny Harris, sipping Coca-cola and watching the flashing lights, said, 'Are you going to have a turn, Vicar?' 'Might boost your collection a bit if you win!' That was the blond tearaway Wayne Atkinson.

'No, I'm not intelligent enough to follow all the combinations of "hold", "nudge" and "gamble" — besides, I'm skint: the churchwardens have been cutting back my pocket-money because the congregations have been pretty poor. Which reminds me, Wayne —'

'I've been going to help my grandad on Sunday mornings, Vicar — honest!' He drew his finger across the front of his skull-and-crossbones T-shirt, crossing his heart and hoping to die, as the saying goes.

'And here was I thinking you were lounging in bed, when all the time you were performing acts of charity!'

'Charity nothing!' said Richard Mulgrove. 'He gets paid for it. Anyhow, he does lie in bed. He never goes to his grandad's workshop 'till twelve o'clock.'

I affected a look of disparaging solemnity. 'O dear, dear! Now what do you think might be a suitable penance for missing church *and* telling tales to the Vicar, eh?'

'Another coke, please!' said Jenny.

Sheepish Wayne shuffled in the direction of the bar. I sat in the old easy chair in the corner. As casually as I could I said, 'What time d'you leave here most nights, then?'

Richard said, 'It depends how much cash we've got. Sometimes half-ten. Sometimes closing.'

'I've got to be in by ten except weekends.' said Jenny.

'Worst thing', said Wayne coming back from the bar 'is when you've got to wheel your motorbike for miles because as soon as that old bat on the corner hears the kick start she comes to the door shouting and screaming.'

'I was going to mention that. I saw Mrs Walton yesterday.' Lugubrious looks all round. 'You know, she lives on her own and old folk get a bit edgy, a bit testy —'

'You're telling me! she said she'd report me to the police for being drunk and disorderly just because I shouted across the road to Angela. I'd only had two Cokes and half of lager.'

Jenny stared flatly into her drink. I got the impression that she and Angela did not see exactly eye to eye over the topic of Wayne. She said, 'That was the night you were showing off the new horn on your bike, though, Wayne. It was that that disturbed the old woman.' No one said anything. There was a cheer from the other side of the room, and the darts match was over.

'Great! Now we can play the jukebox. Have you got a 10p, Wayne?'

'Just for the sake of peace and quiet — you know, when you leave, pipe down a bit eh?'

''Course we will! We always do!' And they ran across to the gleaming jukebox.

I went to the bar and bought a packet of the salty, woody, yeasty straws that I am addicted to. 'Jim having a night off, is he?'

Sally said, 'No, he's at the hospital. I was expecting him back before now. But I suppose, what with the weather and everything . . .'

'Hospital? What, for himself or just visiting?'

'Emergency.' I must have looked startled because she said immediately, 'Well, sort of. Mrs Thingamy on the corner —

the one who always has a lot to say — begging your pardon, Vicar — anyhow, she slipped on her doorstep just as Jim was going out to the warehouse for more lemonades. It's her ankle. Probably just sprained, but you never know. You know what old folks are like. And Jim, he's dead soft. He said straight away: "No use taking any risks and it's pointless asking the ambulance to come out from York this weather — take all day. I'll run her in the car." Mind you, that was half-past four. What time is it now?'

It was ten o'clock. Sally looked harassed and anxious. She fidgetted with the beer mats on the bar and emptied an ashtray that did not need emptying. The darts players were crowding round in search of more drink. Then the door opened and there was an icy wind followed by the overcoated Jim and Mrs Walton in her furs. She looked out of her element, like a missionary falling upon fleshpots. Her nose was a luminous red but her cheeks were pale as ever. There was snow on her fringe.

'Now then, Mrs Walton, a brandy is very warming.' He turned to Sally. 'And I'll have a pint, love, while you're about it.'

And there sat Mrs Walton until closing time with her foot up on a low stool.

'I don't know what I'd have done without Mr Hargreaves.' She was more relaxed than I had ever seen her.

'Jim', said Jim. 'Anyhow, it's not broken. But you'll have to rest it for a week or two.' He turned to Sally who took his empty glass and filled it without remark. 'There was a right old queue in casualty and then there was that lot to cope with.' He gestured towards the black square of window. Then he winked at Mrs Walton and called to the youngsters by the jukebox and the men near the dartboard: 'Last orders, gentlemen, please!'

20

THE SON WHO WAS LOST

'You must have been on your knees all night, Vicar.'

'I beg your pardon! I didn't know I looked as tired out as that!'

An exchange between me and Nancy Rice as we boarded the coach for the parish trip to Bridlington. She was referring to the fact that the sun was beating down out of a cloudless blue.

A last minute check: 'Speak up anyone who's not here!' and we were off. Twenty-five adults and eighteen children, or you might say forty-three children of all ages packed into Lister's forty-one seater. The first fight began as we passed through the outskirts of York. Claire Nelson, aged six, wanted to sit near the window and in the course of wriggling across the seat she had sat on Jeremy Chambers' sandwiches — and his crisps.

'I don't like them all scrunched up! I'm going to hit you!' Thwack. Tears. Tale-bearing Claire running to the back of the bus to tell her mother all about it, but falling as the bus rounded a bend. Screeching of brakes. Screeching from Claire even louder. When one starts they all start. You might have thought they were being taken on a trip to the dentist's. The domestic hell of fractiousness exported from the playgroup to the A64 coast road. A chorus of parents trying out many diversions:

'Let's have a look at this picture book.'

'Here, look what I've got!' Pulls out packet of mints, bar of chocolate, etc.

'Why don't we play that game of spotting number-plates?'

But the children were steadfast, immoveable in their grief. We were only five minutes the other side of York when David Blaney asked, 'Are we nearly there yet?' and Susan Turner said she wanted to go home.

My mind went back to Mary Leonard standing by the lychgate and waving us off: 'Have a good time. I wish I were coming.' I tried a long shot. 'Hush!' I said, 'And I'll tell you a story.' I began to tell them the sentimental tale by Oscar Wilde, *The Selfish Giant*. Soon the children were quiet — some were even asleep. Only the mothers were crying. 'Tell us another!' said Claire, having recovered, thanks to the Oscar Wilde and a hefty vanilla slice. Jeremy, showing what I took to be extraordinary signs of penitence, asked for '. . . the one where Jesus gets left behind in the Temple.' So I told them that story from the second chapter of St Luke.

Was it a trip like this, asked David Blaney, that Jesus and his parents went on? Clearly, he was having thoughts of a Lister's trip to old Jerusalem. This story is always a favourite with children — perhaps because the account of Jesus' staying behind in the Temple without his parents' knowledge sounds to young ears as an act almost bordering on naughtiness: it is easier to identify with this boy Jesus than with the little Goody-Two-Shoes of Victorian piety.

There was no more trouble. Sandwich boxes were duly opened and sandwiches were duly eaten. Lister the driver pointed with the stem of his pipe at landmarks as we passed them. Half a dozen people asked me what time we were to set off back. After the sandwiches there was talk of fish and chips as we all played the game 'first to see the sea'. We parked on the north side of the town, only a hundred yards from the shore. The sea was a flat, misty blue, the perfect reflection of a serene sky. Across the harbour were white hotels in a line like a row of teeth. Further to the north the savage cliffs of Flamborough stood out like a rotting jaw.

The harbour was full of boats and the smell of fish. There were shrieking clouds of gulls around the masts. They were like so many white handkerchiefs waving in the wind. Bridlington resembled a picture postcard of itself.

On the beach a crowd of wary paddlers stood round a marooned jellyfish. There were queues at the chip shops and even longer queues at the whelks and shrimps stalls. I stood by the TEAS tent talking to a man whose face was covered in white whiskers and who was smoking a pipe more acrid than Jack Lister's. After the tea I was buried in the sand by Miss Jessop's Sunday school class who then ran off to get ice-creams. I resurrected myself and got rid of the sand between my toes by joining the paddlers.

Bridlington welcomes careful explorers. I found a shop that sold ancient sepia photographs and cards, a church with a lovely Victorian interior — Gothic Revival before it went mad. And near the church there was a quaint shop called 'The Catholic Repository'. They had plaster figurines of the Pope in the window, irreverently marked 'To Clear'. They looked as if they would pock-mark if you poked them. There was the 1930s 'Hotel Expanse' where I was longing to turn that 'a' into an 'e'. Naturally there were also those eternal monuments of the seaside, the amusement arcades with their flashing, bleeping machines and Muzak, with spellbound teenagers emptying their pockets of tenpenny pieces in order to play the noisy games. They looked uninterested and glum, as if their repetitive actions had been predetermined.

I kept meeting members of our party as I roamed around the town: Miss Jessop and her sister, knees bent, eyes on the little balls, teaching the youngsters pitch and putt; Stephen Wright slurping a towering sundae oblivious to the tugging demands of his little brother who wanted to be taken to the loo; Jack Lister, hands in pockets, a shifty smirk on his face, ducking into the licensed betting shop. I was enjoying the leisure and the relative anonymity, the peculiar pleasure of a visit to a resort with which I was fairly familiar — that of not being quite certain of just what lies round the next corner. There were buskers with guitars near the Post Office and a scary evangelist with a lurid sandwich board by the harbour wall: 'THE END IS NIGH'. For effect he ought to have been standing on the end of the pier. I was about to go into the fresh fish shop, Taste O' the Sea, when Mrs Chambers came running towards me with a look of such terror on her face that I thought she must have been convinced by the grey evangelist.

'Vicar, it's our Jeremy — we've lost him!' She was looking about her in all directions as she spoke, flustered, breathless.

'How long has he been missing?'

'I noticed he was gone about an hour ago. Everybody's searching. D'you think I should get the police?'

So we went to the police station, peering up every alley, glancing into every doorway and arcade as we went. The atmosphere of Bridlington had changed in a moment: the casual, wandering crowds no longer seemed to be innocently at leisure; their mild jostling appeared to us in our anxiety to be malevolence, a conspiracy preventing us from finding Jeremy. We went down the wrong street and so traipsed three sides of a square before we got to the police station.

The sergeant was standing with his hands on his hips making a loud speech at two teenagers with leather trousers and spiky hair. Evidently he was not entirely satisfied with the way they had been riding their motorbike along the front. He waved them away with a warning and they slunk out of the door. Then he looked down into an enormous ledger that covered the whole surface of his desk. He noticed us: 'Sir? Madam? And what can I do for you?' He sounded cheerful. He was smiling. He met our panic with what seemed criminal indolence.

'So he's lost, is he?' The sergeant was so unperturbed. I felt like saying, 'No, he's not lost! Whatever gave you that idea? It's just a game we like to play when we come to Bridlington — provides a bit of work for the coppers!'

'Are you his parents, then?' He opened the ledger at a different page and bit the top off his ballpoint.

'She is.'

'I am.' We both spoke at once. The smile faded and he gave us a vaguely disgusted look.

'So, you've lost him, eh?'

John Cleese would have leapt over the counter and expostulated: 'Not lost, of course not. He's only hiding. Let's see if he's under your tunic!'

The sergeant tested his pen by making an extravagant scribble on a worn blotter. 'Well,' he said, 'it is the getting lost season after all. Your lad's the fifth today.'

I wanted to ask if they had found the other four. The sergeant said, 'Can I have a full description, please?'

Mrs Chambers spoke quickly. The policeman wrote slowly. There was a form to fill in. Then he called out 'Constable Barratt' and a pencil-thin giant of a cadet came up and took the form away. There was the sound of keys turning in a big lock. I imagined hysterically that the constable was about to fetch us a replacement boy out of the cells — one of the four who had been lost but were now found. Then the sergeant began to make polite conversation. It was lovely weather for the time of year. Mind you we deserved it. Bridlington had suffered terribly during the last three wet summers, depending as it did so much on tourism and so on.

Mrs Chambers was distraught. 'Aren't you going to *do* anything, sergeant?'

'Do, madam?' He sounded puzzled, as if someone had

asked him to perform a difficult conjuring trick. Then he added, 'I'm doing all I can. I can't leave this desk to look for the lad myself — I'm on duty you see. But Constable Barratt is informing all officers in the town by radio.' So that was where the angular giant had gone! The sergeant returned to the perusal of his ledger.

Mrs Chambers shuffled frenetically: 'What can we do, officer?'

'Do, madam?' His sang-froid was infuriating. 'There's not much we can do — just keep on looking until the lad's found.'

We were torn between adding to the posse of searchers or hanging on in the station in case any word came through. As if to point up our dilemma, the telephone rang at once. The sergeant picked it up, said the one word 'Yes', then replaced it. We stood aghast. Mrs Chambers began, 'Was that — ?' The sergeant said the one word, 'No'.

The tall cadet came back with cups of tea. We sat. We paced about. We took it in turns to go out among the crowds and search. The day drew on. Cafés filled for high tea. The sun bent to a smaller angle and made the sea sparkle even more brightly. Evening papers were on sale. Still no Jeremy. It was approaching the time we had arranged with Lister for the coach to set off back home.

I went to where we were parked. The adults stood by the coach looking anxious. The children were unnaturally subdued. Jack Lister, not looking as if his time in the bookmaker's had amounted to very much, said, 'What 'ave I to do, Vicar?'

'Well,' I said, all uncertain, 'we'll hang on a bit.'

The town seemed void of policemen so that I wondered if there actually was a force for the cadet to have alerted in the first place. I went towards the harbour and stared into the deep, oily water and thought the worst. The evangelist had

packed up his sandwich board and gone home. When I
returned to the police station, Mrs Chambers was crying
and a lady officer was trying to comfort her with a friendly
arm and more tea. I said, for the umpteenth time, 'Don't
worry, he'll turn up.'

Still, it was as if I had said the wrong thing. She let out a
loud wail and said, 'And the tide's on the way in. What if
he's trapped somewhere, cut off?'

'It's not likely, madam', said the sergeant from behind his
ledger, 'the beach patrol doesn't miss much. Anyone in
danger by the shore gets picked up straight away.'

But Mrs Chambers was not reassured. Someone came in
to report a stolen car. He had to go through the same
procedure we had gone through over Jeremy. There was
nothing much happening for a while: the telephone was
silent, no one came in, no one went out. 'It's usually our
quiet time, early evening. It'll liven up when the pubs turn
out,' said the sergeant gratuitously. No one answered him.
At eight o'clock I sent a message to Lister to tell him to set
off without us.

At eight-fifteen a grinning policeman, who looked even
younger than the pencil-thin cadet, came into the station
with Jeremy. The lad looked perfectly blasé. His mother
rushed across the room and almost crushed him in her
arms. 'Mind my ice cream, Mum!'

Then the words in a continuous flow — a hundred rapid
questions giving Jeremy no time to answer any one of them
before the next one was asked. When he did get the chance
to speak he said, 'When I lost you, Mum, I tried to find you
for a bit. And when I couldn't I went and sat in the church
— like Jesus on that trip he had to Jerusalem.'

'That's where I found him sarge', said the young copper;
'inside St Mark's — fast asleep. I tried the door as I was
passing, routine, like. When it opened I thought I'd just pop

in and sniff about a bit. I was thinking of vandalism. Thought of this young lad never entered my head. Then there he was all curled up on a pew by the font . . .'

It was all smiles and even more tea — the station seemed to run on it. The sergeant remained nonchalant as ever. Soon we returned to the coach — Lister having decided to wait another half hour. The gospel for the first Sunday after Epiphany — our Lord's visit, as a boy, to the Temple — will for ever remind me of Bridlington. Jeremy grew in wisdom and stature, and next year he is to be presented to the Bishop for Confirmation.

21

MORE THINGS IN HEAVEN AND EARTH

When I first arrived in our parish I was reminded that it is Civil War country — I mean by that not the tiffs that break out on the parish council from time to time, but the somewhat larger affair which took place in the middle of the seventeenth century. Our church still wears the scars of soldiers' vandalism. The heavy oak door, fitted in 1633 and referred to, of course, as 'the new door', is lined with sketches of Charles I — etched by the bayonets of bored Roundhead troops who kept their Royalist prisoners in the nave after the 1644 battle. This is damage done thoughtlessly by men who had nothing to do except endure long days and nights of guard-duty; but there are other examples of vandalism performed in the furtherance of a theological doctrine — the smashed stoup, the marks on the north side pillar from where a statue of the Blessed Virgin had been wrenched and mutilated, the ruination of the one small window which used to contain ancient stained glass. Time hallows even our loutishness, and these eyesores have become minor treasures in a way: they are among the first items to be remarked on by our part-time guides when it comes to showing round American tourists. Damage done idly, damage done maliciously; there are also examples of damage done by accident — the fourteenth-century stone skull which was discovered grinning and intact in the churchyard in 1935 and which someone dropped and broke in two in 1936; also an elegant Jacobean lectern which, incredibly, a nineteenth-century sidesman and stoker of the church boiler used as a chopping block. There is a gash in the poor varnished bird's neck; otherwise she has been perfectly restored to her original position and purpose and now stands vigilantly under the hymnboard looking as if she will peck the congregation if they dare fall asleep in the sermon.

Tales of the supernatural are normal in such a place. One of our ladies, putting finishing touches to her display for a flower festival, caught sight of what she took to be a pile of old clothes in the south-west corner. It was dusk and she was alone in the building. She made a note to move the old clothes on her way out. 'But,' she said, 'I suddenly saw the pile of clothes stand up and walk across the back of the church from one side to the other and disappear through the wall. It looked like a soldier and he seemed to be wounded. I didn't stay to finish that pedestal of flowers!'

There was a churchwarden who always stayed back after the morning service to put the kneelers straight and tidy the hymnbooks. As he reached the back pew he became vaguely aware of a figure up in front, standing by the lectern as if searching the huge Bible for a particular lesson. He began a casual conversation with the figure in the unselfconscious way people often do as they are working at some light routine. 'I wondered why I was getting no answer. I thought maybe he was engrossed in looking for his passage in the book. Then, when I'd stacked all the books, I stood up straight and stared at him. It was a monk — cowl over his head and everything! He never made a sound. He walked two or three paces into the middle of the choir and vanished!'

It was Charles Fletcher's favourite story. He would trot it out sooner or later — usually later! — at many a church function. A broad man with a broad and friendly face, a few long strands of black hair across his weathered pate — I imagined them standing on end at the sight of the mysterious monk. The last time he told his tale, I said, 'I'm sure you'd been supping some of your home-brewed churchwardens' ale that day, Charlie.'

But he stuck to his story indignantly: 'Not likely, Vicar — it was only half-past eleven in the morning.' And his eyes opened wide as he added slowly, in his deep voice, 'I saw him, I tell you.' It was the tone that made the choirboys shudder and ask him to tell them the story again.

It was one of the choirboys, Derek Fish, who met me one morning in the vestry and asked, 'D'you think there are such things as ghosts, Vicar?' It was a warm summer morning and the church was filled with sunlight, so the thought of ghosts seemed academic rather than oppressive.

'I don't know, Derek. People say they've seen all sorts of strange things. What do *you* think?'

He was adamant: 'I'm sure there are ghosts. And I'm sure they come to give us a message.'

'Like angels, you mean? That's what "angel" means, you know — "messenger".'

He went rather red. 'Oh, I'm not sure I believe in angels, Vicar.'

'Well, what kind of thing is that to say! You're so certain of ghosts but you're doubtful when it comes to angels. What's the difference?'

There was a picture of huge, winged Gabriel on the vestry wall. It was the Annunciation. He looked stern. Moreover, he seemed not to be looking at Mary but out of the picture and into the room.

It was one of those pictures where the eyes seem to follow you as you move about. Derek gave the picture a nervous glance. He said, 'There are ghosts in the Bible, though, aren't there?'

'A few. But far more angels.'

'Sometimes when I'm in church by myself putting out the hymn lists, I feel as if there's someone watching us. Once there was an old lady sitting at the back. She never made a sound. I hadn't seen her before — ever. I was sure she was a ghost. She just sat there and stared straight ahead. I was scared stiff. Then the church began to fill up. It's a funny thing — I kept looking down into the nave for that old lady all through the service. But I never saw her again. She just vanished!'

'Vanished! Old ladies are often little old ladies. She'd have got hidden behind a big fella like Mr Dale or Mr Ward.'

'But there's more to it than that, Vicar. You know how stuff gets left behind after the service? —'

'Two umbrellas and a pair of gloves last week alone.'

'— Well, when I went out of church that same morning, I noticed a white handkerchief in the pew just where the old lady had been sitting. When I first saw her she was holding a white hanky.'

'That proves it then! She was real enough. Or do your ghosts blow their noses? I'm sure angels don't have to.'

He looked unconvinced. I looked back at stern Gabriel. Derek said, 'It was the atmosphere though. You know, when I looked at the old lady she just seemed so unreal, weird. It wasn't like looking at a real person.'

'No need to be frightened, anyway. If she was unreal she couldn't possibly do you any harm, could she? And if she was a real little old lady she wouldn't do you any harm either. So you were quite safe, whatever.'

At once there was a loud rattling noise. The latch on the vestry door jerked up and down and two of Derek's friends rushed in. Derek and I noticed the startled look in each other's eye and we both smiled. That sudden rattling had done more than all Derek's talk to make me sceptical of my scepticism. I told Barbara the tale when I got home. She said, 'Perhaps it doesn't pay to dismiss ghosts quite so quickly. Remember when we first came here and you used to go across and switch on the boiler last thing on a Saturday night; you weren't keen on that walk through the church-yard, to that old boiler-house.'

'That was because it was always cold and wet.'

She did not say another word.

The following Friday was the evening of the choir's outing to York Minster to hear Bruckner's *Te Deum* and the *Coronation Mass* by Mozart. Music in a huge stone building is the best sound we are likely to hear this side of heaven: it is as fresh and immediate as sparkling wine in heavy cut glass. I thought I was in heaven already.

The performance finished at about half-past nine and we set off to return to Marton by coach. It was warm, sultry even; the sun low in the sky over the flat land, the trees motionless in the sultry air. Mrs Bennett said, 'I think there's going to be a storm, Vicar — if my headache is anything to go by.'

Mr and Mrs Brightside got off at their cottage between two villages and I went up and sat in their seat at the front of the bus. The driver was new at Lister's Coaches, new to the area in fact, and I wanted to make sure he knew about the short cut over Marston Moor. He said, 'Oh yes, thanks. I've had my instructions from Jack.'

Just as he finished speaking I looked ahead out of the panoramic window. Not far ahead, by the roadside, stood a Cavalier, a soldier from the seventeenth-century Civil War. He was in the full colours of his uniform and he wore a real sword. The shock made me shiver as if the blade of that sword was being stroked up and down my spine. I couldn't speak. The driver seemed not to notice the apparition, which never moved, but simply smiled up at the coach as we passed.

In a minute we were disembarking by the lychgate. I felt I

must search out Derek Fish and tell him what I had seen; but he had been at the back of the coach, singing not-quite-respectable songs with the other choirboys all the way home. As they jumped down from the bus they were still involved in their camaraderie and games. I put off the idea of talking to him until Sunday morning. When they had all gone home, I went back inside the coach where the driver was bending among the seats to make sure no one had left anything behind.

'Look,' I said, 'you'll probably think I've gone barmy, but did you see anything on the road back there?'

'See anything?' he replied in that mildly incredulous style which people adopt when they have been asked a stupid question. 'Nothing — except the bloke in the uniform.' He spoke as if the vision had been perfectly natural, as if the ancient soldier had been a present day tommy from the local army camp and his flamboyant uniform had been khaki.

'So you did see him, then?'

'Well, you couldn't miss him, dressed like that, could you?' And he just went on shutting the windows with a matter-of-factness that was definitely this-worldly. I did not know whether to feel more or less frightened. Which was worse — to be unbalanced enough to have hallucinations, or to be unfortunate enough to see ghosts?

'Sealed Knot', said the driver. I thought he was talking about securing the windows. I stood with my mouth open. 'Sealed Knot', he repeated. 'That society that gets together and replays all the old battles. Well, it's Marston Moor Week isn't it?'

Perhaps I could have been excused. It was, as I said, my first year in the parish. And it was Marston Moor Week — the first week in July when the Sealed Knot Society comes to re-enact the 1644 battle. Perhaps the apparition I had seen on the road was one of the advance party come to reconnoitre the country in time for the mock struggle that was to take place the following day? And my terror had been caused by nothing more startling or supernatural than a bank clerk or a solicitor from York enjoying his costumed hobby.

On the Sunday morning I caught young Derek as he was putting up the hymn numbers. I told him my story and ended with the words, 'So you see, it was just an ordinary chap, dressed up.'

'Perhaps', he said. As I went to put on my surplice, the vestry seemed unusually chill for the first week in July.